HTML

Illustrated Brief Edition

Elizabeth Eisner Reding

A DIVISION OF COURSE TECHNOLOGY
ONE MAIN STREET, CAMBRIDGE, MA 02142

an International Thomson Publishing company I(T)P®

Cambridge • Albany • Bonn • Boston • Cincinnati • London • Madrid • Melbourne • Mexico City
New York • Paris • San Francisco • Singapore • Tokyo • Toronto • Washington

HTML — Illustrated Brief Edition is published by CTI

Managing Editor:	Marjorie S. Hunt
Product Manager:	Nicole Jones Pinard
Developmental Editor:	Jessica Evans
Production Editor:	Nancy Ray
Composition House:	GEX, Inc.
Text Designer:	Leslie Hartwell
Cover Designer:	John Gamache

© 1996 by CTI.
A Division of Course Technology — I⟨T⟩P®

For more information contact:
Course Technology
One Main Street
Cambridge, MA 02142

International Thomson Publishing Europe
Berkshire House 168-173
High Holborn
London WCIV 7AA
England

International Thomson Publishing GmbH
Königswinterer Strasse 418
53227 Bonn
Germany

Thomas Nelson Australia
102 Dodds Street
South Melbourne, 3205
Victoria, Australia

International Thomson Publishing Asia
211 Henderson Road
#05-10 Henderson Building
Singapore 0315

Nelson Canada
1120 Birchmount Road
Scarborough, Ontario
Canada M1K 5G4

International Thomson Publishing Japan
Hirakawacho Kyowa Building, 3F
2-2-1 Hirakawacho
Chiyoda-ku, Tokyo 102
Japan

International Thomson Editores
Campos Eliseos 385, Piso 7
Col. Polanco
11560 Mexico D.F. Mexico

Trademarks

Course Technology and the open book logo are registered trademarks of Course Technology.

I⟨T⟩P® The ITP logo is a registered trademark of International Thomson Publishing.

Netscape Navigator is a trademark of Netscape Communications.

Some of the product names and company names used in this book have been used for identification purposes only and may be trademarks or registered trademarks of their respective manufacturers and sellers.

Disclaimer

Course Technology reserves the right to revise this publication and make changes from time to time in its content without notice.

ISBN 0-7600-4608-5

Printed in the United States of America

10 9 8 7 6 5 4 3 2

From the Illustrated Series Team

At Course Technology we believe that technology will transform the way that people teach and learn. We are very excited about bringing you, instructors and students, the most practical and affordable technology-related products available.

The Development Process

Our development process is unparalleled in the educational publishing industry. Every product we create goes through an exacting process of design, development, review, and testing.

Reviewers give us direction and insight that shape our manuscripts and bring them up to the latest standards. Every manuscript is quality tested. Students whose backgrounds match the intended audience work through every keystroke, carefully checking for clarity and pointing out errors in logic and sequence. Together with our own technical reviewers, these testers help us ensure that everything that carries our name is as error-free and easy to use as possible.

The Products

We show both how and why technology is critical to solving problems in the classroom and in whatever field you choose to teach or pursue. Our time-tested, step-by-step instructions provide unparalleled clarity. Examples and applications are chosen and crafted to motivate students.

The Illustrated Series Team

The Illustrated Series Team is committed to providing you with the most visual introduction to microcomputer applications. No other series of books will get you up to speed faster in today's changing software environment. This book will suit your needs because it was delivered quickly, efficiently, and affordably. In every aspect of business, we rely on a commitment to quality and the use of technology. Each member of the Illustrated Series Team contributes to this process. The names of all our team members are listed below.

Cynthia Anderson
Chia-Ling Barker
Donald Barker
Laura Bergs
David Beskeen
Ann Marie Buconjic
Rachel Bunin
Joan Carey
Patrick Carey
Sheralyn Carroll
Pam Conrad
Mary Therese Cozzola
Carol Cram
Kim Crowley
Linda Eriksen
Jessica Evans
Lisa Friedrichsen
Michael Halvorson
Meta Hirschl
Jane Hosie-Bounar
Marjorie Hunt

Steven Johnson
Nancy Ludlow
Tara O'Keefe
Harry Phillips
Nicole Jones Pinard
Katherine Pinard
Kevin Proot
Nancy Ray
Elizabeth Eisner Reding
Neil Salkind
Gregory Schultz
Ann Shaffer
Roger Skilling
Dan Swanson
Marie Swanson
Jennifer Thompson
Sasha Vodnik
Jan Weingarten
Christie Williams
Janet Wilson

Preface

Welcome to *HTML – Illustrated Brief Edition*. This highly visual book offers new users a hands-on introduction to HTML and also serves as an excellent reference for future use.

Organization and Coverage

This text contains four units and three appendices that cover basic HTML skills. In these units students learn how to create a Web page using HTML, format the page, add graphics to the page, and create forms. The appendices offer a handy reference to locating and using HTML resources.

About this Approach

What makes the Illustrated approach so effective at teaching software skills? It's quite simple. Each skill is presented on two facing pages, with the step-by-step instructions on the left page, and large screen illustrations on the right. Students can focus on a single skill without having to turn the page. This unique design makes information extremely accessible and easy to absorb, and provides a great reference for after the course is over. This hands-on approach also makes it ideal for both self-paced or instructor-led classes. The modular structure of the book also allows for great flexibility; you can cover the units in any order you choose.

Each lesson, or "information display," contains the following elements:

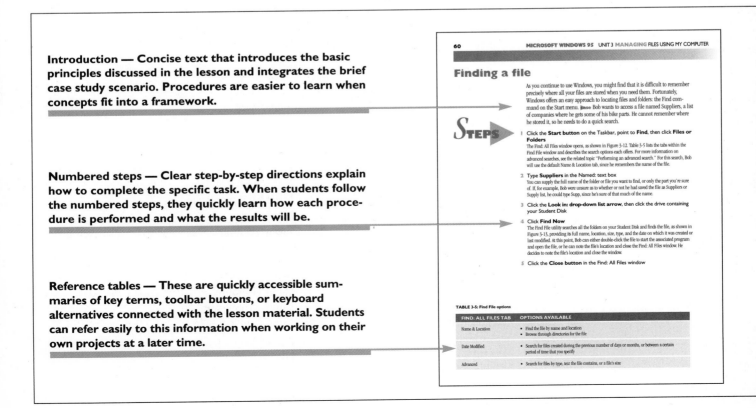

Introduction — Concise text that introduces the basic principles discussed in the lesson and integrates the brief case study scenario. Procedures are easier to learn when concepts fit into a framework.

Numbered steps — Clear step-by-step directions explain how to complete the specific task. When students follow the numbered steps, they quickly learn how each procedure is performed and what the results will be.

Reference tables — These are quickly accessible summaries of key terms, toolbar buttons, or keyboard alternatives connected with the lesson material. Students can refer easily to this information when working on their own projects at a later time.

---

60   MICROSOFT WINDOWS 95   UNIT 3 MANAGING FILES USING MY COMPUTER

Finding a file

As you continue to use Windows, you might find that it is difficult to remember precisely where all your files are stored when you need them. Fortunately, Windows offers an easy approach to locating files and folders: the Find command on the Start menu. Bob wants to access a file named Suppliers, a list of companies where he gets some of his bike parts. He cannot remember where he stored it, so he needs to do a quick search.

STEPS

1. Click the **Start button** on the Taskbar, point to **Find**, then click **Files or Folders**
   The Find: All Files window opens, as shown in Figure 3-12. Table 3-5 lists the tabs within the Find File window and describes the search options each offers. For more information on advanced searches, see the related topic "Performing an advanced search." For this search, Bob will use the default Name & Location tab, since he remembers the name of the file.

2. Type **Suppliers** in the Named: text box
   You can supply the full name of the folder or file you want to find, or only the part you're sure of. If, for example, Bob were unsure as to whether or not he had saved the file as Suppliers or Supply list, he could type Supp, since he's sure of that much of the name.

3. Click the **Look in: drop-down list arrow**, then click the drive containing your Student Disk

4. Click **Find Now**
   The Find File utility searches all the folders on your Student Disk and finds the file, as shown in Figure 3-13, providing its full name, location, size, type, and the date on which it was created or last modified. At this point, Bob can either double-click the file to start the associated program and open the file, or he can note the file's location and close the Find: All Files window. He decides to note the file's location and close the window.

5. Click the **Close button** in the Find: All Files window

TABLE 3-5: Find File options

FIND: ALL FILES TAB	OPTIONS AVAILABLE
Name & Location	• Find the file by name and location • Browse through directories for the file
Date Modified	• Search for files created during the previous number of days or months, or between a certain period of time that you specify
Advanced	• Search for files by type, text the file contains, or a file's size

Other Features

The two-page lesson format featured in this book provides the new user with a powerful learning experience. Additionally, this book contains the following features:

- Read This Before You Begin HTML – This page provides essential information that both students and instructors need to know before they begin working through the units.

- Real-World Case – The case study used throughout the textbook is designed to be "real-world" in nature and representative of the kinds of activities that students will encounter when using HTML to create Web pages. With a real-world case, the process of solving the problem will be more meaningful to students.

- End of Unit Material – Each unit concludes with a Task Reference that summarizes the various methods used to execute each of the skills covered in the unit. The Task Reference is followed by a meaningful Concepts Review that tests students' understanding of what they learned in the unit. The Concepts Review is followed by a Skills Review, which provides students with additional hands-on practice of the skills they learned in the unit. The Skills Review is followed by Independent Challenges, which pose case problems for students to solve. The Independent Challenges allow students to learn by exploring and develop critical thinking skills. The Visual Workshops that follow the Independent Challenges also help students to develop critical thinking skills. Students are shown completed tasks and are asked to recreate them from scratch.

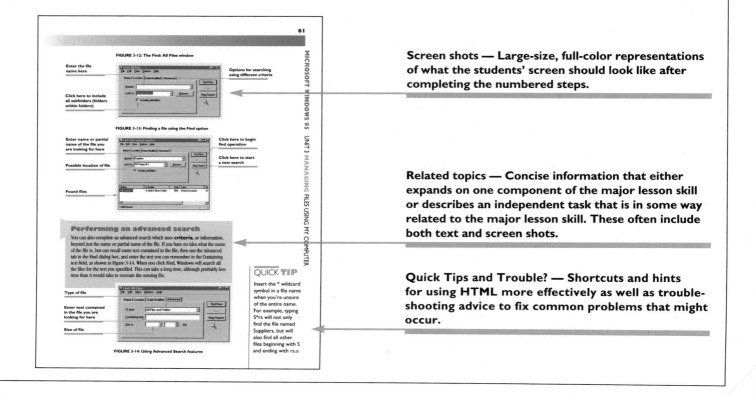

CourseTools

CourseTools are Course Technology's way of putting the resources and information needed to teach and learn effectively into your hands. With an integrated array of teaching and learning tools that offer you and your students a broad range of technology-based instructional options, we believe CourseTools represents the highest quality and most cutting edge resources available to instructors today. CourseTools can be found at http://coursetools.com. Briefly, the CourseTools available with this text are:

Student Disks

To use this book students must have a Student Disk. See the inside front or inside back cover for more information on the Student Disk. Adopters of this text are granted the right to post the Student Disk on any stand-alone computer or network.

Course Online Faculty Companion

This new World Wide Web site offers Course Technology customers a password-protected Faculty Lounge where you can find everything you need to prepare for class. These periodically updated items include lesson plans, graphic files for the figures in the text, additional problems, updates and revisions to the text, links to other Web sites, and access to Student Disk files. This new site is an ongoing project and will continue to evolve throughout the semester. Contact your Customer Service Representative for the site address and password.

Course Online Student Companion

Our second Web site is a place where students can access challenging, engaging, and relevant exercises. They can find a graphical glossary of terms found in the text, an archive of meaningful templates, software, hot tips, and Web links to other sites that contain pertinent information. We offer student sites in the broader application areas as well as sites for specific titles. These new sites are also ongoing projects and will continue to evolve throughout the semester.

Instructor's Manual

This is quality assurance tested and includes:
- Solutions to all lessons and end-of-unit material
- Unit notes which contain teaching tips from the author
- Extra Independent Challenges
- Transparency Masters of key concepts

Solutions Files

These files have been quality assurance tested and contain solutions to all end-of-unit material and extra Independent Challenges.

Contents

HTML

Read This Before You Begin HTML

To the Student

The lessons and exercises in this book feature files available on a Student Disk. For information on getting a copy of the Student Disk, refer to the inside front or inside back cover of this book. See your instructor or technical support person for further information.

Using Your Own Computer

If you are going to work through this book using your own computer, you need a computer system running Microsoft Windows 3.1 or later, any Web browser, any text editor, and a Student Disk. The exercises in this book are written using WordPad and Netscape Navigator 2.0 for Windows 95. However, Windows 3.1, other text editors, and other Web browsers will work. You will not be able to complete the step-by-step lessons and exercises in this book using your own computer until you have the Student Disk.

To the Instructor

The Student Disk contains the files students need to complete the step-by-step lessons in the Units, Skills Reviews, Independent Challenges, and Visual Workshops. For information on getting a copy of the Student Disk, refer to the inside front or inside back cover of this book. As an adopter of this text, you are granted the right to distribute the files on the Student Disk to any student who has purchased a copy of this text. You are free to post all files to a network or standalone workstations, or simply provide copies of the Student Disk to your students. The instructions in this book assume the students know which drive and directory contain the Student Disk, so it's important that you provide disk location information before the students start working through the Units.

The instructions also assume that the students are familiar with the World Wide Web and Windows. Although this text is written using Windows 95, WordPad, and Netscape Navigator 2.0, prior versions of Windows, other text editors, and other Web browsers can also be used to complete the lessons in the Units. It is not necessary for students to have an Internet connection to complete the exercises in this book. In most cases, lessons are completed using files on the Student Disk or fictitious Web sites.

UNIT 1

Creating
AN HTML DOCUMENT

Y ou already know how to navigate the World Wide Web. Now you'll learn how to create beautiful Web pages using markup codes called HTML. You'll also learn how to link Web sites, include graphic images and sound files, and create user-friendly forms. ▶case As the Web manager for the Nomad Ltd travel and sporting goods company, Grace Dekmejian needs to create an attractive series of pages that will ultimately allow customers to place orders using the World Wide Web. ▶

Understanding HTML

HTML is an acronym for HyperText Markup Language. It allows all types of computers to interpret information on the World Wide Web in the same way. HTML is a series of tags, sometimes called **elements**, **containers**, or **codes**, that surround text much like parentheses or quotation marks. ▶ Text in an HTML document can be controlled, just as in word processing, by adding formatting attributes such as bolding. In addition, you can insert graphic images, sound files, and multimedia clips that a Web user can click to access. Figure 1-1 shows a Web page created using HTML. ▶**ase** Grace wants Nomad Ltd's Web site to look professional and be easy to use so customers can find what they're looking for. By using an HTML Web page, she can:

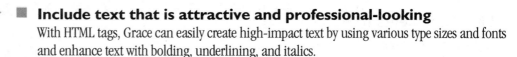

▪ **Include text that is attractive and professional-looking**
With HTML tags, Grace can easily create high-impact text by using various type sizes and fonts and enhance text with bolding, underlining, and italics.

▪ **Link Web sites**
In your own experience using the Web, you've probably gone from one location to another using links. **Links**, or hyperlinks, are other Web site addresses (called uniform resource locators or URLs) that are coded into an HTML document. Since Nomad cooperates in a variety of environmental projects, Grace will include links to take readers directly to information that may be of interest to them. The ability to link Web sites—even those not belonging to Nomad—lets Grace create an informative, easy-to-use series of pages. As URLs change, she can continuously update and modify these links. Figure 1-2 shows the relationships that can exist between Web pages.

▪ **Create tables and lists**
Grace can use HTML to create numbered and bulleted lists. In addition, tables can be created to make columnar text or data easy to read.

▪ **Include graphic images, sound files, and multimedia clips**
Web pages without graphic images would be dull, and Grace wants Nomad's Web site to be exciting and interesting to visit. She wants to include plenty of graphic images and sound files.

FIGURE 1-1: Web page created using HTML

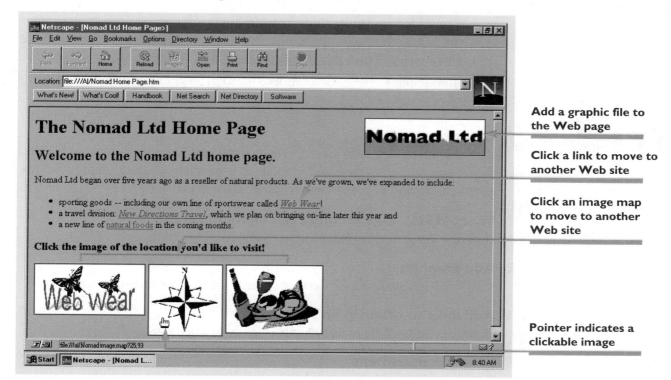

Add a graphic file to the Web page

Click a link to move to another Web site

Click an image map to move to another Web site

Pointer indicates a clickable image

FIGURE 1-2: Possible relationships between Web pages

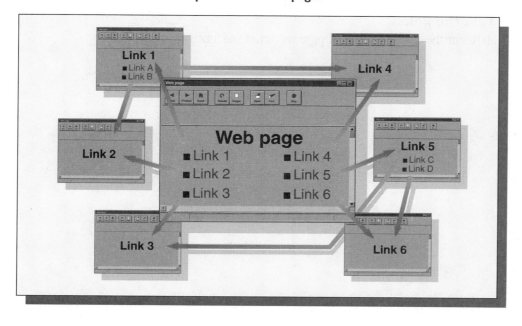

Planning an HTML document

Before writing an HTML document, you should plan what elements you want on the page. Although you'll probably modify your initial page format, it is a good idea to have a master plan. **case** Grace reviews the steps for planning and creating her Web page:

I **Create an outline**
The first step in creating a Web page is to prepare an outline. The outline should include a list of all the elements for your page, including its title, an introductory paragraph, links to other sites, an optional graphic image, and a contact address, as shown in Figure 1-3.

2 **Insert HTML tags around each element on the page**
Type HTML tags around the elements in your outline.

3 **Add graphics**
Insert HTML-compatible graphic files to add value to your page and make it attractive.

4 **Add links to other Web sites**
Create links to other Web sites that would be of interest to your readers.

5 **Save the document**
Save your work often to prevent loss of data.

6 **View the page**
Periodically examine your page using a Web browser, such as Netscape Navigator, which is shown in Figure 1-4. Correct any errors as you go.

7 **Test the links**
Make sure the links in your HTML page are correct and function properly.

FIGURE I-3: Sample outline of a Web page

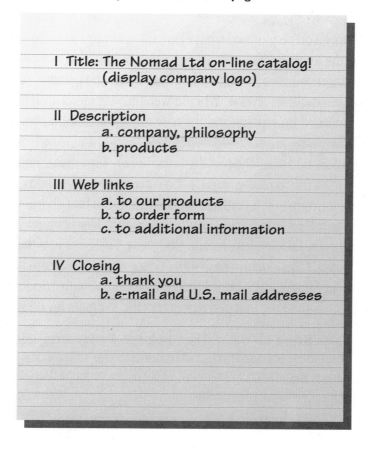

I Title: The Nomad Ltd on-line catalog!
   (display company logo)

II Description
   a. company, philosophy
   b. products

III Web links
   a. to our products
   b. to order form
   c. to additional information

IV Closing
   a. thank you
   b. e-mail and U.S. mail addresses

FIGURE I-4: Completed Web page

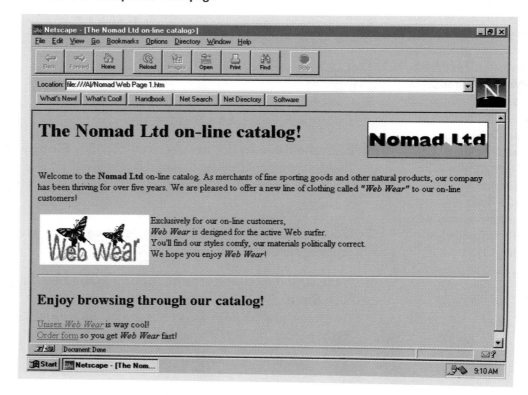

Writing an HTML document

Once you've planned what elements you want to include in your document, it's time to create it. Any word processor can be used to type an HTML document. When you save the document, make sure the document type is a text file using the extension **.htm**. When a Web browser views an HTML document, it ignores uncoded line spaces and the case of tags. HTML tags can be written in upper- or lowercase, are enclosed in brackets (< >), and sometimes occur in pairs (both before and after the text they surround). Tags that do not occur in pairs are sometimes called **empty containers**. The ending tag differs from the beginning tag: it contains a slash (/) as the first character within the brackets. Every HTML document contains tags that identify it as an HTML document, and tags for the Head, Title, and Body text. Table 1-1 lists the tags necessary for a basic HTML document. **case**   Grace decides to create her HTML document using the WordPad word processor included with Windows 95. You can use any word processor that can save a text file to create an HTML document.

This replaces Steps 1, 6, 7, and 8.
1 Double-click the
   Accessories group icon
   to open it, then double-click
   the **Write application
   icon** to open it and maximize
   the screen, if necessary
6 Click the **Drives list
   arrow** then click a:
7 Type **Nomad.htm** in the
   File Name text box
8 Make sure **Text
   Document** appears in the
   Save File as Type list box,
   then click **OK**

1 Click **Start** on the taskbar, point to **Programs**, point to **Accessories**, then click **WordPad**, and maximize the screen, if necessary
A blank WordPad document opens. Grace begins by typing the initial HTML tag at the location of the blinking insertion point.

2 Type **<HTML>** then press **[Enter]**
The typed text appears and the insertion point moves to the next line. Grace finishes typing the text for her document.

3 Type the remaining text shown in Figure 1-5
Now that the initial text is entered, Grace wants to save her work.

4 Insert your Student Disk into the appropriate drive

5 Click **File** on the menu bar, then click **Save**
The Save As dialog box opens. See Figure 1-6.

6 Click the **Save in list arrow**, then click 3½ **Floppy (A:)**
These lessons assume that your Student Disk is in drive A. If you are using a different drive or storing your practice files on a network, click the appropriate drive. Next, Grace types the name of the file.

7 Double-click **Document** in the File name box, then type **Nomad.htm** to replace the default filename

8 Make sure **Text Document** appears in the Save as type list box, then click **Save**
The Save As dialog box closes, and the filename appears in the title bar at the top of the document.

FIGURE I-5: WordPad document with HTML tags

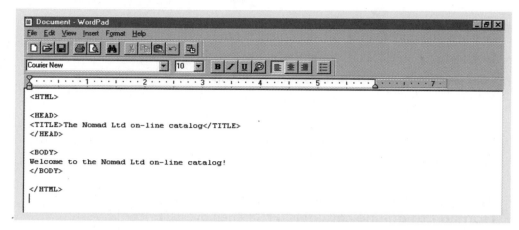

FIGURE I-6: Save As dialog box

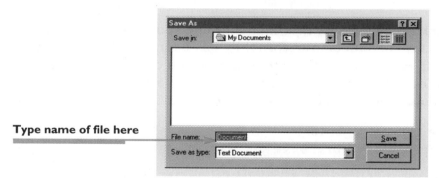

Type name of file here

QUICK **TIP**

HTML is easier to read and write in WordPad if the Wrap to ruler option is selected on the Text tab in the Options dialog box. ▶ You can use upper- and lowercases, line spaces, and hard returns to make your HTML code easier to read without affecting its appearance on the Web. ■

TABLE I-I: Tags in a basic HTML document

TAGS	PURPOSE	EXAMPLE
<HTML></HTML>	Identifies the document as one consisting of HTML tags. Without these tags, the document could be misinterpreted as "text only."	<HTML><HEAD><TITLE>The Nomad Ltd on-line catalog</TITLE></HEAD><BODY>We hope you love our merchandise!</BODY></HTML>
<HEAD></HEAD>	Contains the document's title.	<HEAD><TITLE>The Nomad Ltd on-line catalog</TITLE></HEAD>
<TITLE></TITLE>	Indicates the document's title, which appears in the title bar, and is often used by Web indexing systems.	<TITLE>The Nomad Ltd on-line catalog</TITLE>
<BODY></BODY>	Contains the bulk of the document, including headings, text, lists, links, graphics, and multimedia.	<BODY>We hope you love our merchandise!</BODY>

Editing and viewing an HTML document

Like any document, an HTML document is rarely written perfectly the first time. When editing an HTML document, you use the same editing techniques used in word processing. HTML documents can have up to six sizes of headings. Although each Web browser can display headings differently, Table 1-2 shows the relative size of HTML headings. ▶**case** Grace wants to expand the body text in her document and add headings to give impact to text. She begins the body of the page with a large heading.

1 Place the insertion point before the word **Welcome**, type **<H1>The Nomad Ltd on-line catalog!</H1>**, then press **[Enter]**
Before entering additional text, she wants to delete the exclamation point following the "Welcome" sentence.

2 Place the insertion point after the exclamation point in the next sentence, press **[Backspace]**, then type a period (**.**)
Next, Grace wants to add a short paragraph about Nomad Ltd.

3 Press **[Spacebar]**, type **As merchants of fine sporting goods and other natural products, our company has been thriving for over five years. We are pleased to offer a new line of clothing called "Web Wear" to our on-line customers!**, then press **[Enter]**
Grace needs to add a new paragraph using the <P> tag to explain more about Web Wear.

4 Type **<P>** then press **[Enter]**
Now that the paragraph has been added, she types the new text.

5 Type **Exclusively for our on-line customers. Web Wear is designed for the active Web surfer. You'll find our styles comfy and our materials politically correct. We hope you enjoy Web Wear!**, then press **[Enter]**
Next, Grace wants to add a level 2 heading.

6 Type **<H2>Enjoy browsing through our catalog!</H2>**, then press **[Enter]**
Compare your document with Figure 1-7. Satisfied with her work, Grace saves the file.

7 Click the **Save button** 🖫 on the toolbar
Once her document is saved, Grace views the document in Netscape Navigator.

8 Start Netscape Navigator then open the Nomad file on your Student Disk
Note: You do not have to be on-line to complete the steps. Compare your page with Figure 1-8. Grace leaves Netscape Navigator open so she can easily see her progress, and returns to WordPad.

9 Click the **WordPad program button** on the taskbar

FIGURE 1-7: New text and headings added

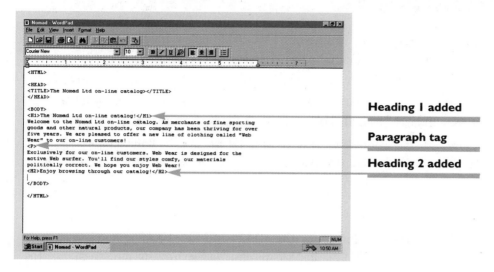

Heading I added

Paragraph tag

Heading 2 added

FIGURE 1-8: Document viewed in Netscape Navigator

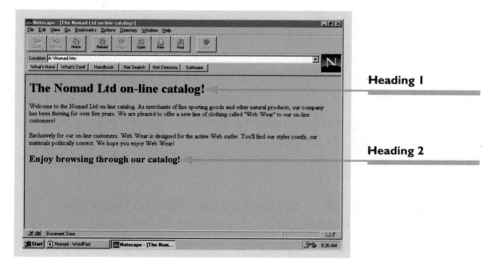

Heading I

Heading 2

TABLE 1-2: HTML headings

HEADING TAGS	SAMPLE	RESULT
<H1> </H1>	<H1>Heading 1</H1>	# Heading I
<H2> </H2>	<H2>Heading 2</H2>	## Heading 2
<H3> </H3>	<H3>Heading 3</H3>	### Heading 3
<H4> </H4>	<H4>Heading 4</H4>	#### Heading 4
<H5> </H5>	<H5>Heading 5</H5>	##### Heading 5
<H6> </H6>	<H6>Heading 6</H6>	###### Heading 6

Linking documents to other Web sites

One of the most exciting features of HTML documents is the ability to go from one Web site to another by clicking a link. **Links**, or **hyperlinks**, are jumps to other Web sites that display on a page in a different color. When the mouse pointer is over a link, it changes to 🖑. Links can be created using URL or local file addresses and can be created before the link file is even created. You may notice that familiar DOS symbols look different in HTML. See the related topic "Translating DOS symbols to HTML" for more information. ▶**case** Grace wants to add two links to the document: one to a page showing different styles, and a second one to an order form page.

I Place the insertion point under the **<H2> </H2>** heading line
Each link will refer to an HTML file that you will create later and save on the Student Disk. The link is defined in the first <A> tag. The information between the first and second tags is what displays, and clicking it moves you to the site.

2 Type **<A HREF=file:///a ⏐ /Nomad2.htm>Unisex Web Wear</A> is way cool!**, then press **[Enter]**
On a real Web page, you would not link files to a disk drive, but to other sites on the Web. In these steps, you will link files to the drive containing your Student Disk. Grace creates a second link to an order form page.

3 Type **<A HREF=file:///a ⏐ /Nomad3.htm>Order now</A> to get Web Wear fast.**, then press **[Enter]**
Compare your document with Figure 1-9. Grace saves her work and switches to Netscape Navigator to view the links.

4 Click the **Save button** 🖫 on the toolbar, then click the **Netscape Navigator program button** on the taskbar
Netscape Navigator becomes active. Since this file is already open, Grace refreshes, or reloads, the image to see the latest changes.

5 Click the **Reload button** 🔄 on the toolbar
The image is updated to display the links added to the file. When the pointer passes over the link, it changes to 🖑, and the site displays in the status area of the browser.

6 Move 🖑 over the text **Order now**, *but don't click the mouse button*
Compare your document with Figure 1-10. Grace returns to the WordPad document.

7 Click the **WordPad program button** on the taskbar

FIGURE 1-9: Links added

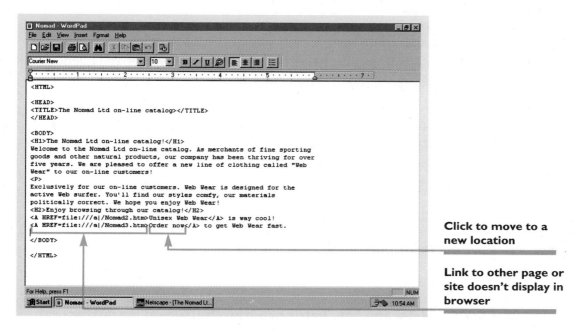

Click to move to a new location

Link to other page or site doesn't display in browser

FIGURE 1-10: Links displayed in the Web page

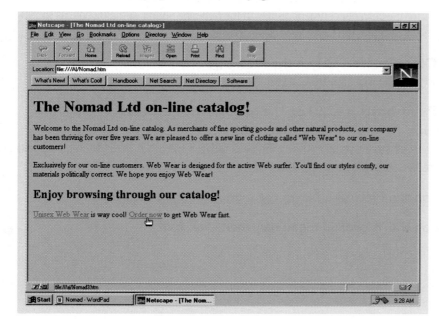

Translating DOS symbols to HTML

Symbols such as the backslash (\ ) and colon (:) look different in an HTML document. The backslash, used to indicate filename locations, is replaced with a slash (/). The colon, used to note a storage volume—such as a diskette—is replaced with a pipe (|). That's why the statement "file:\\\a:\Nomad.htm" was typed as "file:///al/Nomad2.htm." This change in symbols enables a wide range of computers to understand the link.

QUICK **TIP**

Use HTML to create an attractive interface for all your pages, such as a directory, by linking local files.■

TROUBLE?

If your links aren't working, make sure you've changed the \ and : symbols and that your links are typed correctly.■

Printing an HTML document

To keep records of your work, it's important to be able to print documents. Due to their tags, HTML documents are not very attractive; however, you might need to give a co-worker a copy of a document, or you might want to keep a copy for your records. Netscape Navigator makes it possible to view the HTML tags of the active document from within the browser. A Web browser can be assigned to whichever HTML editor you use. See the related topic "Assigning a Web browser to an HTML editor" for more information. ▶case   Grace wants to print the WordPad HTML document and the Netscape Navigator page.

I   Click the **Print button** 🖨 on the toolbar
A single copy of the document prints. Grace decides to view the HTML tags from Netscape Navigator.

2   Click the **Netscape Navigator program button** on the taskbar

3   Click **View** on the menu bar, then click **Document Source**
The HTML tags for the current document display in the Netscape Source of dialog box, as shown in Figure 1-11. After reading the tags, Grace closes the dialog box.

4   Click the **Close button** ❎ on the Netscape Source of title bar
Grace wants to print the Web page using a button on the toolbar.

5   Click the **Print button** 🖨 on the toolbar, then click **OK** in the Print File dialog box
The active page is sent to the printer. Grace is finished with her initial work on this Web page and decides to close Netscape Navigator and WordPad.

6   Click **File** on the Netscape Navigator menu bar, then click **Exit**

7   Click **File** on the WordPad menu bar, then click **Exit**

FIGURE 1-11: HTML tags displayed in Netscape Navigator

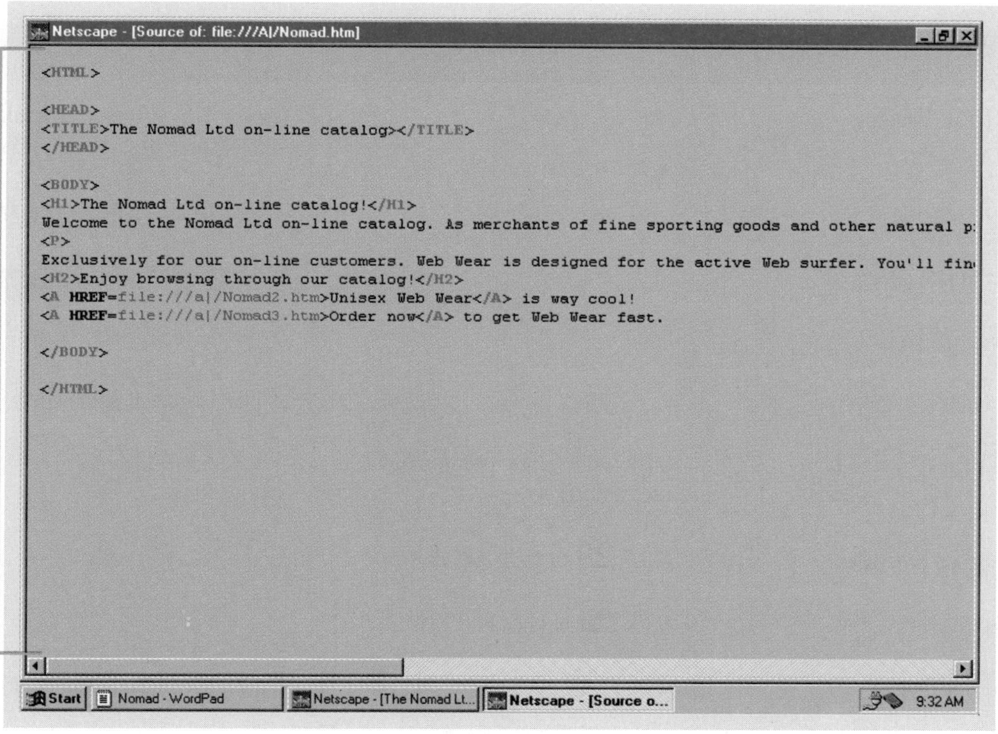

```
Netscape - [Source of: file:///A|/Nomad.htm]                                    _ | 8 | X

<HTML>

<HEAD>
<TITLE>The Nomad Ltd on-line catalog</TITLE>
</HEAD>

<BODY>
<H1>The Nomad Ltd on-line catalog!</H1>
Welcome to the Nomad Ltd on-line catalog. As merchants of fine sporting goods and other natural p
<P>
Exclusively for our on-line customers. Web Wear is designed for the active Web surfer. You'll fin
<H2>Enjoy browsing through our catalog!</H2>
<A HREF=file:///a|/Nomad2.htm>Unisex Web Wear</A> is way cool!
<A HREF=file:///a|/Nomad3.htm>Order now</A> to get Web Wear fast.

</BODY>

</HTML>
```

HTML tags for active Web page display here

Start | Nomad - WordPad | Netscape - [The Nomad Lt... | Netscape - [Source o... | 9:32 AM

Assigning a Web browser to an HTML editor

In the HTML Assistant Pro, your favorite Web browser can be easily assigned to test your current HTML document. Click File on the menu bar, then click Select test browser name. The Test program is dialog box opens. Locate the Web browser you want to use as the test program, as shown in Figure 1-12, then click OK. Once the test program is defined, click the Test button in the HTML Assistant Pro document window to view the document in the browser.

Location of the current test program displays here

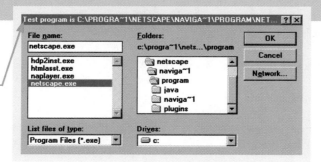

FIGURE 1-12: Assigning a test program in HTML Assistant Pro

QUICK **TIP**

If you have assigned an HTML Editor in Netscape Navigator's General Preferences, the source will be displayed in that editor, not in the Source of window.

▶ You can close a program quickly by clicking the Close button on the program's title bar.■

TASKREFERENCE

TASK	MOUSE/MENU	KEYBOARD
Add an HTML heading		Type <H1> </H1> tags around the heading text; use H1 for largest heading; H6 for smallest heading
Add an HTML title		Type <Title> </Title> tags around the title text
Create a link to a local file		Type <A HREF=file:///al/*filename.htm*>*text*</A>
Create a link to a URL		Type <A HREF=http://*www.location.com*>*text*</A>
Create a new paragraph		Type <P> tag at point where new paragraph should occur
Edit HTML text	Click text to place insertion point, use editing keys	Press [↑] [↓] [←] [→] to position cursor, use editing keys
Exit Netscape Navigator	Click ☒ or click File, Exit	
Exit WordPad	Click ☒ or click File, Exit	
Insert HTML tags		Type tags using open brackets (<) and close brackets (>)
Move from Netscape Navigator to WordPad	Click 🗎 Nomad - WordPad	
Move from WordPad to Netscape Navigator	Click 🗎 Netscape - [The Nomad Lt...	
Open WordPad	Click Start, point to Programs, point to Accessories, click WordPad	
Print HTML document in Netscape Navigator	Click 🖶 Print or click File, Print	[Ctrl][P]
Print HTML document in WordPad	Click 🖶 or click File, Print	[Ctrl][P]
Reload a Netscape Navigator image	Click 🔄 Reload or click View, Reload	
Save a WordPad document	Click 💾 or click File, Save	[Ctrl][S]
Select WordPad Wrap to ruler option	Click View, Options, Wrap to ruler, OK	
View a link in Netscape Navigator	Move pointer over link	
View HTML document in Netscape Navigator	Launch Netscape Navigator, click File, Open File	Launch Netscape Navigator, [Ctrl][O]
View HTML source in Netscape Navigator	Click View, Source	[Alt][V][S]

CONCEPTSREVIEW

Label each element of the WordPad screen shown in Figure 1-13.

FIGURE 1-13

Match each statement with the term or button that it describes.

6 Reloads a Netscape Navigator image

7 Displays an HTML link in Netscape Navigator

8 Prints a WordPad document

9 Displays HTML tags in Netscape Navigator

10 Opens the active WordPad document

a. Nomad - WordPad

b. View, Source Document

c. Reload

d.

e.

Select the best answer from the list of choices.

11 Which tags are used to create the largest heading?

a. <H6> </H6>

b. <Lheading> </Lheading>

c. <H1> </H1>

d. <H1> <\H1>

12 When typing HTML tags, you should type the tags using

a. uppercase only

b. lowercase only

c. either upper- or lowercase

d. uppercase for the opening tag; lowercase for the closing tag

13 Which menu command is used to open a local file in Netscape Navigator?

a. File

b. Edit

c. View

d. Format

14 In HTML, which symbol replaces the colon (:) used in a DOS filename address?

a. /

b. ;

c. }

d. |

SKILLSREVIEW – HW

1 Start WordPad.

a. Open a blank WordPad document.

b. Become familiar with the toolbar buttons.

c. Make sure the Wrap to ruler radio button is selected.

2 Write an HTML document.

a. Type the initial <HTML> tag at the beginning of the document.

b. Type the remaining information shown in Figure 1-14.

c. Save your work as a text document called Crystal Clear Opticals.htm on your Student Disk. *Note for Step 2c: Windows 3.1 users will need to create file-names that are no more than eight characters in length. For example, "Crystal.htm" would substitute in Step 2c.*

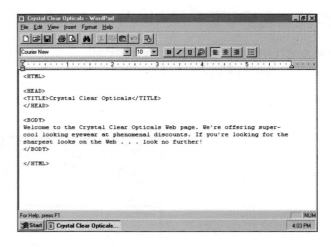

FIGURE 1-14

3 Edit and view an HTML document.

a. Add "Home Page" to the end of the Title text.

b. Add the largest possible heading after the initial Body tag that says "The Crystal Clear Opticals Web page."

c. Add a paragraph tag after ". . . look no further!".

d. Type a new paragraph as follows: "Crystal Clear Opticals has been in business since 1972, and has always been dedicated to offering the best looking eyewear at the lowest prices."

e. Add a smaller size heading under the previous paragraph that says "We know you'll find an attractive style to suit your needs!"

f. Save your work.

g. Open Netscape Navigator then open and view the Crystal Clear Opticals.htm file.

h. Leave Netscape Navigator open then return to WordPad.

4 Link documents and sites.

a. Create a link to a file on your Student Disk called Women's fashions.htm. The clickable text should read "Women, check these out!"

b. Create a link to a file on your Student Disk called Men's fashions.htm. The clickable text should read "Hey, Men, great looking shades!"

c. Save your work.

d. Return to Netscape Navigator and refresh the Crystal Clear Opticals.htm file.

5 Print an HTML document.

a. Print the Netscape Navigator document.

b. View the HTML tags while in Netscape Navigator.

c. Return to WordPad then print the Crystal Clear Opticals document.

d. Exit WordPad.

e. Exit Netscape Navigator.

f. Submit your printed materials.

INDEPENDENT — HW
CHALLENGE 1

Your computer consulting business, Star Dot Star, now has a "Web presence." Using the skills you learned in this unit, plan and create a Web page for your consulting firm. Use WordPad to write your HTML tags, then use Netscape Navigator (or whichever browser is available) to view the finished page. Your page should include at least two headings, as well as links to other Web pages or sites.

To complete this independent challenge:

1 Create an outline that includes all the topics you want to cover in your Web page.

2 Decide which HTML tags you'll need and which outline elements they'll be assigned to.

3 Decide if you'll want to use any graphic images, which you'll insert at a later date. Where will you insert these images?

4 Add at least two links to your Web page.

5 Save your work as a text document called My Web Page.htm on your Student Disk.

6 Print the document in WordPad and in Netscape Navigator.

7 Submit your printed materials.

INDEPENDENT
CHALLENGE 2

Your local Board of Realtors has hired you to create a Web page for your community. Because you are familiar with the area and HTML, you'll be able to design a professional-looking page that will help attract potential real estate customers.

To complete this independent challenge:

1 Create an outline that includes all the items you want to include in your Web page. What qualities about your community do you want to mention?

2 Decide which HTML tags you'll need and which outline elements they'll be assigned to.

3 Decide if you'll want to use any graphic images, which you'll insert at a later date. Where will you insert these images?

4 Add at least three links on your Web page.

5 Save your work as a text document called Real Estate.htm on your Student Disk.

6 Print the document in WordPad and in Netscape Navigator.

7 Submit your printed materials.

VISUALWORKSHOP

Use the skills you learned in this unit to create the Web page shown in Figure 1-15. Save your HTML file on your Student Disk in WordPad as a text document called Marvelous Musicals.htm, then print the document in WordPad and Netscape Navigator. Submit your printed materials.

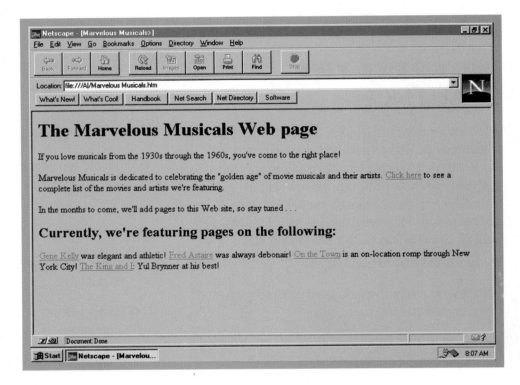

FIGURE I-I5

- ▶ Plan document formats
- ▶ Create lists
- ▶ Add text enhancements
- ▶ Use preformatted text
- ▶ Create a table

Controlling
HTML TEXT

Now that you know how to create a simple Web page and link sites to it, it's time to learn how to control the text within it. You can format HTML text in many ways to make it more attractive and dynamic when viewed with a Web browser. ▶case Grace wants to enhance the text on Nomad Ltd's Web page to attract customers to visit other Nomad sites. ▶

Planning document formats

HTML documents can contain a variety of formatted text. As you learned previously, a Web document's appearance is controlled by its HTML tags. These tags control whether the text has numbers or bullets before each line, and how each level of the text is indented or displayed. Common HTML formats found in Web documents are shown in Table 2-1. **case**   Grace decides how she wants her text to appear on the page. Using common HTML tags, she can display her text using:

■ **Ordered lists**

Sometimes referred to as a *numbered list*, each line of text in the list is preceded by a number. If Grace decides to change the order of the items in the list, HTML will automatically renumber the list correctly.

■ **Unordered lists**

Each item in an unordered or *bulleted list* is preceded by a dark, round circle, as shown in Figure 2-1. Each item in an unordered list displays with a hanging indent, in which each new line of the text appears directly underneath the previous line. Grace will use an unordered list to call attention to specific products.

■ **Directory lists**

Like a telephone directory, a directory list appears as multiple columns across a Web page. This type of list is used to display items of equal importance in a wide, space-saving format.

■ **Menu lists**

Items in a menu list display left-justified one beneath another; they contain neither numbers nor bullets, and have no hanging indent. This type of list is appropriate when displaying related items that don't have any special order.

■ **Definition lists**

A definition list, also shown in Figure 2-1, is a handy way of displaying a term or short group of words with an indented description under each term.

■ **Nested lists**

Most outlines contain not only headings, but subheadings as well. A nested list allows you to create expanded ordered and unordered lists by combining their tags within an existing list.

FIGURE 2-1: Web page with sample lists

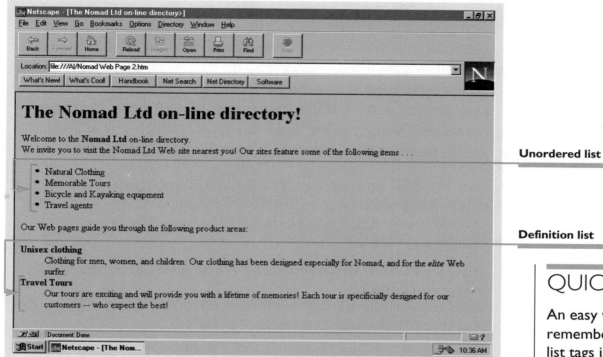

Unordered list

Definition list

TABLE 2-1: Common HTML formats

DESCRIPTION	TAGS	DESCRIPTION	TAGS
Ordered list	<OL> <LI>*Item 1*</LI> <LI>*Item 2*</LI> </OL>	Unordered list	<UL> <LI>*Item 1*</LI> <LI>*Item 2*</LI> </UL>
Directory list	<DIR> <LI>*Item 1*</LI> <LI>*Item 2*</LI> </DIR>	Menu list	<MENU> <LI>*Item 1*</LI> <LI>*Item 2*</LI> </MENU>
Definition list	<DL> <DT>*Item 1*</DT> <DD>*description*</DD> <DT>*Item 2*</DT> <DD>*description*</DD> </DL>	Nested list	<OL> <LI>*Item A*</LI> <UL> <LI>*Item 1*</LI> <LI>*Item 2-a*</LI> <LI>*Item 2-b*</LI> </UL></OL>

Creating lists

Arranging text in a list format is an effective way of displaying information. Depending on how it's arranged, a document with one or more lists can be easier to read than one with text in paragraph form. You can use an ordered list to show items of varied importance; an unordered list works well for displaying text of equal importance. ►ase   Grace wants to organize her Web page so customers can easily see Nomad's on-line items. She's already started her HTML document and has inserted placeholders where she wants the lists to occur.

I   **Start WordPad, open the file HTML 2-1.htm on your Student Disk, then save it as Nomad2.htm**
Grace starts her ordered list by typing the <OL> initial tag. A selected placeholder is automatically replaced by typing.

2   **Select the PLACE ORDERED LIST HERE placeholder, type <OL>, then press [Enter]**
Each of the individual items in the list must be surrounded by the HTML tags <LI> and </LI>. Grace types the first item in the list and its tags.

3   **Type <LI>Mega way-cool bitmapped T-Shirt</LI>, then press [Enter]**
Grace adds the remaining items to the list of the available designs.

4   **Type the remaining three items highlighted in Figure 2-2, then press [Enter]**
Conclude the ordered list using the </OL> HTML tag.

5   **Type </OL> then press [Enter]**
Next, Grace uses a definition list to explain each of the designs. Unlike the ordered list, the definition list uses three groups of HTML tags. The initial definition tag is <DL>.

6   **Select the PLACE DEFINITION LIST HERE placeholder, type <DL>, then press [Enter]**
A definition list consists of a text line, usually containing the term to be defined. The definition, or explanation, appears indented on the line beneath the term.

7   **Type <DT>Mega way-cool bitmapped T-Shirt</DT>, then press [Enter]**
In the next line of text, Grace types the definition. Then she'll end the definition list and finish it later.

8   **Type <DD>An original creation, 100% cotton, in navy blue or crimson.</DD>, press [Enter], type </DL>, then press [Enter]**
Compare your document with Figure 2-2.

9   **Save your document, start Netscape Navigator, then view the Nomad2.htm file and scroll through the file to view all the lists**
Compare your work with Figure 2-3. Continue to the next lesson.

Word

Definition

FIGURE 2-2: HTML document with ordered and definition list tags

Type these tags for
ordered list

Tags for definition list

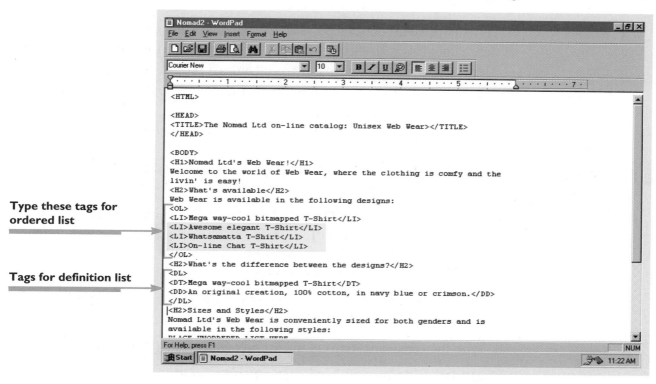

FIGURE 2-3: Web page with ordered and definition lists

Ordered list

Definition list

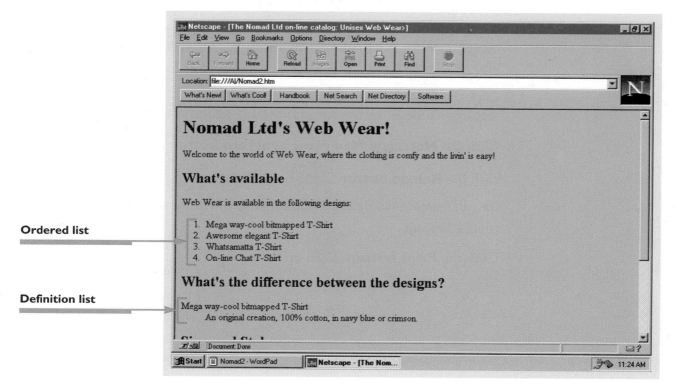

Creating lists, continued

An unordered list makes it possible to display text with bullet characters preceding each line. This is an effective way of calling attention to each line. An unordered list is created in the same manner as an ordered list, except that the initial and final tags are <UL> and </UL>. **case** Grace wants to include an unordered list on her Web page. She begins by activating the HTML document in WordPad, but leaves Netscape Navigator open so she can review her progress.

10 Click the **WordPad program button** on the taskbar
The Nomad2.htm document appears. Grace begins by typing the initial unordered list tag.

11 Select the **PLACE UNORDERED LIST HERE** placeholder, type **<UL>**, then press **[Enter]**
As in an ordered list, each of the individual items in the list are surrounded by the HTML tags <LI> </LI>. Next, Grace types the first item in the list and its tags.

12 Type **<LI>Long sleeves, crew neck</LI>**, then press **[Enter]**
Grace types the remaining items in the list of available designs.

13 Type the remaining items in the list below pressing [Enter] after each line:

<LI>Long sleeves, turtleneck</LI> [Enter]

<LI>Short sleeves, crew neck</LI> [Enter]

<LI>Short sleeves, turtleneck</LI> [Enter]

Grace finishes her unordered list with the </UL> tag.

14 Type **</UL>** then press **[Enter]**
Compare your completed HTML document with Figure 2-4. Now that her lists are complete, Grace saves her work.

15 Click the **Save button** 🖫 on the toolbar
Next, Grace decides to view her document in Netscape Navigator.

16 Click the **Netscape Navigator program button** on the taskbar, then click the **Reload button** on the toolbar

Compare your page with Figure 2-5; you might have to scroll down the screen. Grace decides to print the Web page.

17 Click the **Print button** on the toolbar

FIGURE 2-4: Tags for unordered list

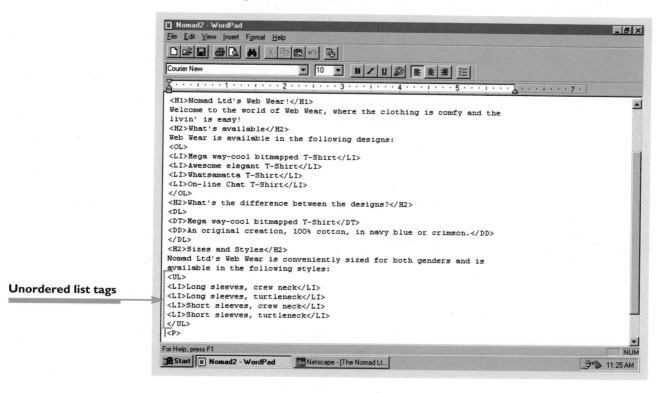

Unordered list tags

FIGURE 2-5: Unordered list in Netscape Navigator

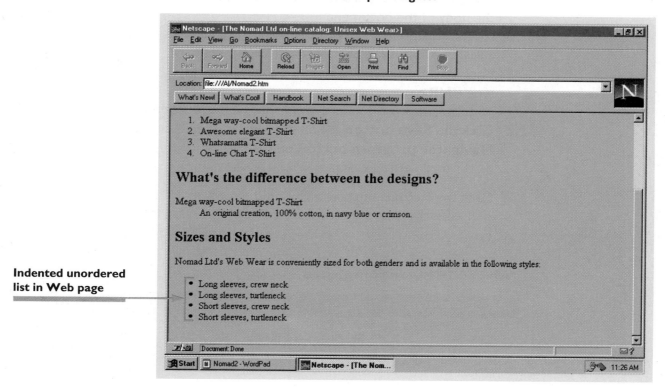

Indented unordered list in Web page

Adding text enhancements

You can enhance text in an HTML document by adding formatting tags for bolding, italics, and underlining (although some Web browsers do not display underlining). Most HTML formatting tags must surround the text they enhance, however, not all HTML tags require this. By typing a single tag, you can create a dividing line (also known as a horizontal rule) to separate items on the screen, or a line break to force a line to end before the right margin. Table 2-2 lists some common HTML formatting tags. See the related topic "Physical versus logical tags" for more information. ▶**case**   Grace wants to enhance the text in her Web page to make it look more attractive. She'll insert additional HTML tags in the existing WordPad document.

1   Click the **WordPad program button** on the taskbar
Grace wants the words "Web Wear" in the initial heading in the document to be in italics.

2   Place the insertion point to the left of the word **Web** in the first heading in the body of the text, then type **<I>**
Grace adds the final italics tag after the word "Wear."

3   Place the insertion point to the right of the word **Wear** in the first heading in the body of the text, then type **</I>**
Since the words "Web Wear" are generally in italics whenever the product line is printed, Grace decides to add italics tags around each occurrence throughout the document, *except within the title tags*.

4   Complete Steps 2 and 3 for every occurrence of the words **Web Wear** in the body of the document
Compare your document with Figure 2-6. To separate the introductory text from the "What's available" heading, Grace adds a horizontal rule to the page.

5   Place the insertion point after "… the livin' is easy!", press **[Enter]**, then type **<HR>**
After making these changes, Grace views the document in Netscape Navigator.

6   Click the **Save button** 🖫 on the toolbar, then click the **Netscape Navigator program button** on the taskbar
Next Grace reloads the document in Netscape Navigator.

7   Click the **Reload button** ⟳ Reload on the toolbar
The modified Web page appears, as shown in Figure 2-7. Continue to the next lesson.

TABLE 2-2: HTML text formatting tags

DESCRIPTION	TAG(S)	DESCRIPTION	TAG(S)
Boldface text	<B> </B>	Italicize text	<I> </I>
Underline text	<U> </U>	Line break	
Horizontal rule	<HR>		

FIGURE 2-6: Italics tags added to document

Italics tags in document

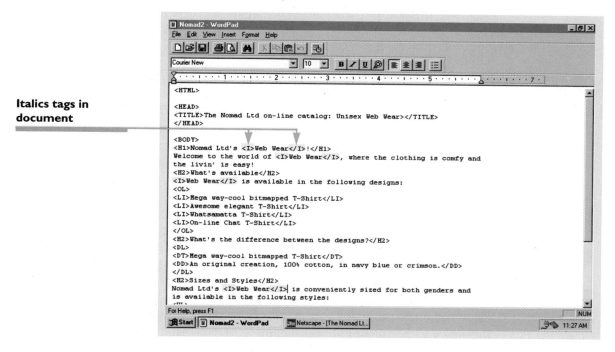

FIGURE 2-7: Modified text in Netscape Navigator

Horizontal rule

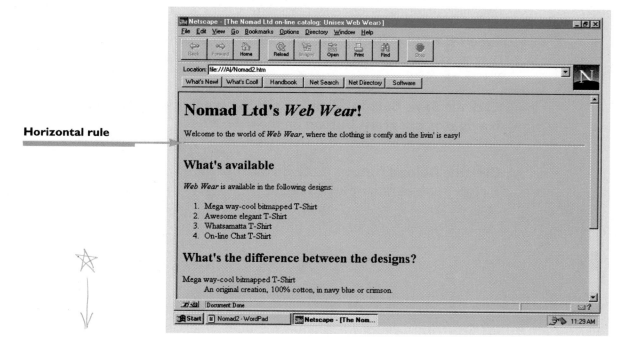

Physical versus logical tags

In the past, HTML used *logical* tags to enhance text to define a level of enhancement, rather than a particular look, and the Web browser determined the text appearance. In most cases, using EM displayed text in italics and STRONG displayed text in bold. *Physical* tags such as <B>, <I>, and <U> identify exactly how text will look.

Adding text enhancements, continued

Sometimes you might want to end a line to make the text look more attractive. A line break is used to end a line of text manually. **case**   Before she completes the rest of her modifications, Grace returns to the WordPad document.

8 Click the **WordPad program button** on the taskbar
In most cases, the width of your Web browser window determines when a line of text wraps around to a new line. The
 HTML tag lets you control where a new line of text will begin when displayed in a Web browser. Grace thinks the introductory text will have more impact if it appears on two lines.

9 Place the insertion point after the space that follows "Welcome to the world of <I>Web Wear</I>," in the first heading, type **
, then press **[Enter]
To make the names of the designs of the products stand out, Grace decides to display the names as bold text.

10 Place the insertion point to the left of the word **Mega**, then type **<B>**
To complete the bold process, she adds the final tag after the text.

11 Place the insertion point after the word **bitmapped**, then type **</B>**
Grace makes the names of each of the designs bold.

12 Type **<B>** and **</B>** tags around each of the designs
Compare your document with Figure 2-8. Grace saves her work and switches to Netscape Navigator to view the changes.

13 Click the **Save button** 🖫 on the toolbar, then click the **Netscape Navigator program button** on the taskbar
Netscape Navigator becomes active. Grace reloads the document to see the latest changes.

14 Click the **Reload button** 🔄 on the toolbar
The page is updated, as shown in Figure 2-9.

FIGURE 2-8: Line break and bold tags added to document

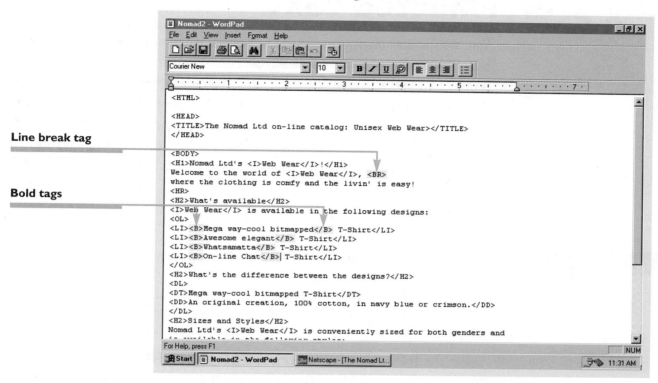

Line break tag

Bold tags

FIGURE 2-9: Web page with line break and bold enhancements added

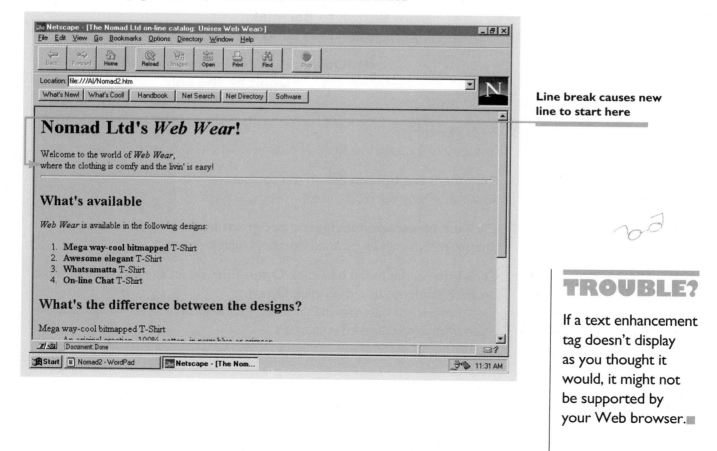

Line break causes new line to start here

TROUBLE?

If a text enhancement tag doesn't display as you thought it would, it might not be supported by your Web browser. ■

Using preformatted text

Your Web browser determines how HTML tags are interpreted and how formatted text, such as bold, italics, and bulleted lists will look when displayed. Since there are a variety of browsers currently in use, there is a possibility your text won't look quite the way you want. For that reason, it's possible to include preformatted text in your HTML document. The text within the preformatted tags (<PRE> </PRE>) will be spaced exactly the way you type it in your document. For more information on entering HTML tags such as <PRE>, see the related topic "Using an HTML editor." ▶**case**   Grace wants to make sure text in her Web page is displayed exactly as she types it.

1 Open the WordPad document HTML 2-2.htm, then save it as Nomad3.htm on your Student Disk
Preformatted text can include enhancements, such as bolding and italics, and allows you to include your own line spaces and breaks without having to include the <P> and
 HTML tags inserted in regular text. Grace wants to include preformatted text in her document.

2 Select the **INSERT PREFORMATTED TEXT HERE** placeholder, then type the following text exactly as follows, pressing [Tab] to indent the lines and [Enter] to insert line breaks and blank lines as needed

   <PRE>Web surfers
   from Boston to Bermuda
   love <I>Web Wear</I>!

   <B>Quick . . . order yours now!!!</B>
   Don't be the only surfer without
   <I>Web Wear</I>! </PRE>

3 Press [Enter]
Compare your document with Figure 2-10. Before viewing the document, Grace saves her work.

4 Click the **Save button** 🖫 on the toolbar
Now Grace wants to view her document in Netscape Navigator.

5 Click the **Netscape Navigator program button** on the taskbar
Since this file is not already displayed, she opens it using the menu.

6 Click **File** on the menu bar, click **Open File**, select the Nomad3.htm file on your Student Disk, then click **Open**
The Web page appears, as shown in Figure 2-11. Grace is satisfied with her work and wants to make further modifications to her document.

FIGURE 2-10: HTML tags for preformatted text

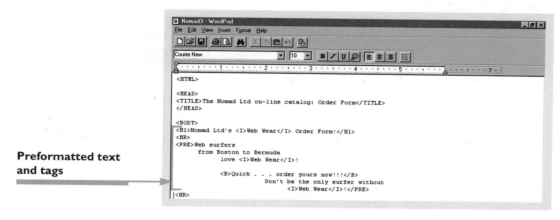

Preformatted text and tags

FIGURE 2-11: Preformatted text displayed in Netscape Navigator

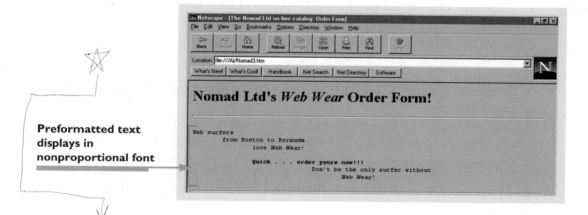

Preformatted text displays in nonproportional font

Using an HTML editor

You can make the process of writing HTML code easier by using one of the many HTML editors available. These editors can usually be downloaded from an FTP site and make creating HTML documents very easy. Instead of having to type various tags, you can insert the tags around selected text by clicking a toolbar button. See Figure 2-12 for an example of an HTML editor called HTML Assistant Pro. For information about downloading an HTML editor, see the Appendix.

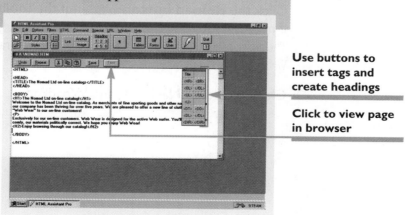

Use buttons to insert tags and create headings

Click to view page in browser

FIGURE 2-12: Document in the HTML Assistant Pro

Creating a table

One of the ways the <PRE> HTML tag can be used is to create a table. A table is created using the preformatted text tags, by typing the text exactly the way you want it to display on the page. Most text on a Web page displays in proportional type (such as Times New Roman), but preformatted text displays in nonproportional type (such as Courier) *exactly* as it is typed, including line breaks and spacing. Some Web browsers support an HTML tag designed specifically for tables (<TABLE> </TABLE>). Since these tags are not supported by all Web browsers, it's safer to use preformatted text. See the related topic "Using <TABLE> tags to create tables" for more information. ▶case   Grace wants to add a table to the WordPad document that shows the colors available for each design.

1   Click the **WordPad program button** on the taskbar
A placeholder already exists in the document. Grace will replace the placeholder with preformatted text that will contain the table. Since she wants the column titles to be bold, she types the bold tag immediately after the preformatted tag.

2   Select the **INSERT TABLE HERE** placeholder, type **<PRE><B>**, then press **[Enter]**
Grace wants customers to see the available colors for each design. When creating a table, you can control the space between columns better if you use the Spacebar rather than the Tab key, since the Spacebar allows you to create an exact amount of space between columns.

3   Type the table data shown in Figure 2-13, then press **[Enter]**
Once the table data is typed, Grace types the final preformatted text tag.

4   Type **</PRE>** then press **[Enter]**
Now that she's finished entering the table text, Grace saves her work.

5   Click the **Save button** 🖫 on the toolbar
Next, Grace switches to Netscape Navigator.

6   Click the **Netscape Navigator program button** on the taskbar
The active document appears. Since changes have been made, she reloads the document.

7   Click the **Reload button** 🗘 on the toolbar, then scroll down the page, if necessary, to see the preformatted text
The active page is displayed, as shown in Figure 2-14. Grace is finished with her work on this Web page and closes Netscape Navigator and WordPad.

8   Close Netscape Navigator and WordPad

FIGURE 2-13: Table data entered as preformatted text

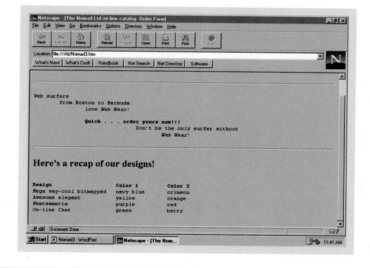

Preformatted tags surround table data

Use the Spacebar to create space between columns

FIGURE 2-14: Completed table in Netscape Navigator

Using <TABLE> tags to create tables

For browsers that support the <TABLE> tags, this is a much easier way to create professional-looking tables. A bordered table is surrounded with the <TABLE BORDER> </TABLE> tags, and uses the <TR> </TR> tags to define each row within the table. Data in each cell in a row is surrounded by the <TD> </TD> tags, and is displayed as bold and centered using the <TH> </TH> tags (for headings, for example). Figure 2-15 shows a table created using TABLE tags.

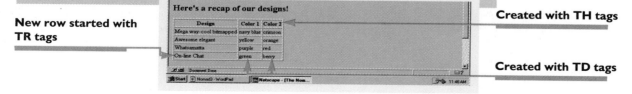

New row started with TR tags

Created with TH tags

Created with TD tags

FIGURE 2-15: Table with border created with TABLE tags

TASKREFERENCE

TASK	KEYBOARD
Add items to a definition list	Type <DT>*item*</DT>; type <DD>*definition*</DD>
Add items to an ordered, unordered, directory, definition, menu, or nested list	Type <LI>*text*</LI>
Bold text	Type <B>*text*</B>
Create a definition list	Type <DL>*text*</DL>
Create a directory list	Type <DIR>*text*</DIR>
Create a horizontal rule	Type <HR>
Create a line break	Type
Create a menu list	Type <MENU>*text*</MENU>
Create a table row	Type <TR>*text*</TR>
Create a table with a border	Type <TABLE BORDER>*text*</TABLE>
Create an ordered list	Type <OL>*text*</OL>
Create an unordered list	Type <UL>*text*</UL>
Create emphasized text	Type <EM>*text*</EM>
Create preformatted (table) text	Type <PRE>*text*</PRE>
Create strong text	Type <STRONG>*text*</STRONG>
Create table data	Type <TD>*text*</TD>
Create table headings	Type <TH>*text*</TH>
Italicize text	Type <I>*text*</I>
Underline text	Type <U>*text*</U>

CONCEPTSREVIEW

Label each element of the WordPad screen shown in Figure 2-16

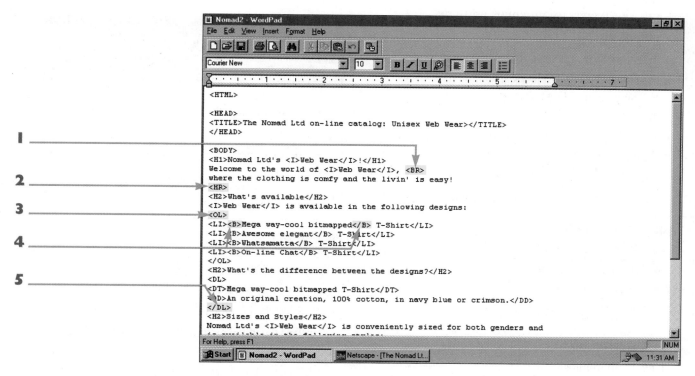

FIGURE 2-16

Match each statement with the HTML tags it describes.

6 Opening and closing preformatted text tags

7 Opening and closing italics tags

8 Opening and closing list item tags

9 Opening and closing underline tags

10 Opening and closing menu list tags

a. <U> </U>

b. <PRE> </PRE>

c. <MENU> </MENU>

d. <I> </I>

e. <LI> </LI>

Select the best answer from the list of choices.

11 Which tag(s) are used to create a horizontal rule?

a.

b. <HR></HR>

c. <RL>

d. <HR>

12 Which key do you press to create column spaces when typing preformatted text?

a. [Spacebar]

b. [Tab]

c. either [Spacebar] or [Tab]

d. [Ctrl]

SKILLSREVIEW ~ HW ~

1 Create a list.

  a. Start WordPad and open the file HTML 2-3.htm on your Student Disk, then save it as Interstellar Pizza.htm.

  b. Select the INSERT UNORDERED LIST HERE placeholder.

  c. Type the initial unordered list tag, then press [Enter].

  d. Type the text for the list items, including the beginning and ending HTML tags, as shown in Table 2-3.

  e. Press [Enter] after all the items are typed, then type the ending HTML unordered list tag.

  f. Save your work. *as Intersteller Pizza.htm*

  g. View the document in Netscape Navigator.

TABLE 2-3: Interstellar Pizza
<LI>imported cheeses</LI>
<LI>organically grown ingredients</LI>
<LI>farm-fresh crust</LI>
<LI>organic spices</LI>

2 Add text enhancements.

  a. Return to WordPad.

  b. Bold the text "Interstellar on-line pizzeria!".

  c. Italicize each of the remaining headings.

  d. Add a horizontal rule in the line above the heading "Nothing but the best for you!".

  e. Create a line break after the space that follows "We make the finest pizza".

  f. Save your work.

  g. Reload the changes to the document in Netscape Navigator.

3 Use preformatted text.

  a. Return to WordPad.

  b. Select the INSERT PREFORMATTED TEXT HERE placeholder.

  c. Type the initial preformatted text tag, then press [Enter].

  d. Type the preformatted text shown in Figure 2-17.

  e. Press [Enter] after the last line of preformatted text, type the closing preformatted text tag, then press [Enter].

  f. Save your work.

  g. Reload the changes to the document in Netscape Navigator.

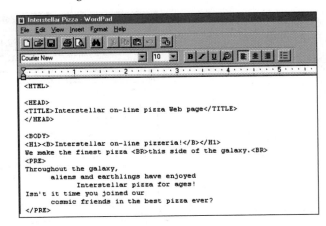

FIGURE 2-17

4 Create a table.

  a. Return to WordPad.

  b. Select the INSERT TABLE HERE placeholder.

  c. Type the initial preformatted text tag, then press [Enter].

  d. Type the text shown in Table 2-4.

  e. Type the closing preformatted text tag on a new line below the table.

  f. Type the opening bold tag after the opening preformatted text tag.

  g. Type the closing bold tag after "Size."

  h. Save your work.

  i. Print the WordPad document.

  j. Reload the changes to the document in Netscape Navigator.

  k. Print the Netscape Navigator page.

  l. Close and exit Netscape Navigator and WordPad.

TABLE 2-4: Table text		
Pizza Type	Topping(s)	Size
Safety zone	cheese	10" and 14"
Surfer's special	pepperoni, onions	6" and 14"
Alien madness	onions, garlic, sausage	14"
Planetary revenge	SURPRISE!!!	6", 10", and 14"

INDEPENDENT
CHALLENGE 1 – HW –

The Star Dot Star computer consulting firm is ready to expand its Web page. Using the document you previously created, expand it by adding lists and text formatting. Your page should contain at least two types of lists, and some text formatting such as bolding or italicizing.

To complete this independent challenge:

1 Start WordPad, open the file My Web Page.htm that you created in Unit 1, then save it as Star Dot Star-page 1.htm on your Student Disk.

2 Add a definition list that defines the types of services you provide.

3 Add an unordered list that describes the types of clients you have.

4 Add horizontal rules, line breaks, and text formatting where appropriate.

5 Print the document in WordPad.

6 Print the document in Netscape Navigator.

7 Submit your printed materials.

INDEPENDENT
CHALLENGE 2

Your work with your local Board of Realtors continues. They have been very happy with your initial work on their Web page, and they would like for you to add text enhancements and lists to the existing page.

To complete this independent challenge:

1 Start WordPad, open the file Real Estate.htm that you created in Unit 1, then save it as Realtors-1.htm on your Student Disk.

2 Identify at least three geographic regions where houses are sold in your area, then create a definition list that identifies where these houses are located for prospective customers.

3 Use a definition list to describe the three regions you listed in Step 2.

4 Add text enhancements where appropriate to add impact to the page.

5 Save your work.

6 Print the document in WordPad.

7 Print the document in Netscape Navigator.

8 Submit your printed materials.

INDEPENDENT
CHALLENGE 3

You've recently opened your own video store, Film Clips, and you've decided to design an in-store information system that uses HTML and Netscape Navigator. With this system, customers can learn more about the movies in the store. Film Clips specializes in your favorite kind of movies—horror, comedies, recent blockbusters—whatever you like.

To complete this independent challenge:

1 Open a blank WordPad document and save it as a text document called Film Clips-1.htm on your Student Disk.

2 Design an outline for your store's Web page.

3 Include a list of the types of movies available in your store on the page.

4 Include a list of some of the prominent stars featured in these films.

5 Add text enhancements where appropriate to add impact to the page.

6 Save your work.

7 Print the document in WordPad.

8 Print the document in Netscape Navigator.

9 Submit your printed materials.

INDEPENDENT
CHALLENGE 4

You have been hired to design a Web page for a local astrologer, Madam Zylog. Madam Zylog reads horoscopes and tells fortunes. She specializes in palmistry, or reading a person's fortune, and wants to emphasize that she is particularly gifted in predicting a person's economic and romantic future.

To complete this independent challenge:

1 Create an outline that includes all the items you want to include in this Web page.

2 Start WordPad, open a new document, then save it as a text document called Madam Zylog-1.htm on your Student Disk.

3 Include at least two types of lists in this page.

4 Include text enhancements where necessary to add impact to the page.

5 Save your work.

6 Print the document in WordPad.

7 Print the document in Netscape Navigator.

8 Submit your printed materials.

VISUALWORKSHOP *homework   so back to Ch.1*

Use the skills you learned in this unit to create the Web page shown in Figure 2-18. Save your HTML file on your Student Disk in WordPad as a text document called Barbara's Bakery.htm, then print the document in WordPad and Netscape Navigator.

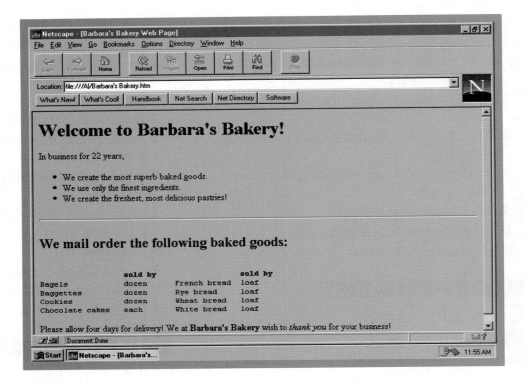

FIGURE 2-18

UNIT 3

OBJECTIVES

- ▶ Understand graphic images
- ▶ Use inline graphics
- ▶ Link graphics
- ▶ Create image maps
- ▶ Insert multimedia files

Adding
GRAPHICS AND MULTIMEDIA

W hile text conveys the message in your Web page, pictures can add spice and pizzazz. In an HTML document, pictures are inserted as graphic images or electronic art files that are displayed by your Web browser. **case** Grace wants to include Nomad's logo and other graphic images to make Nomad's Web pages more attractive and interesting. ▶

Understanding graphic images

When a graphic image, or picture, is displayed on a Web page, it is not actually saved in the HTML source document. You can display a graphic image in a Web browser by using HTML tags to point to its location. Graphic images are available in a variety of formats, and most images can be viewed by Web browsers. Some graphic images are displayed *natively* by browsers (meaning they are displayed without additional assistance); other graphic images, however, are not supported natively (they require the *external* assistance of helper programs). The most common graphic image file formats supported by Web browsers are shown in Table 3-1. **case**   Grace considers what options she has when using graphic images in her Web documents:

Use common file formats

A GIF image is the most common natively supported graphic file format and can be displayed by most graphics-capable Web browsers. GIF images work well for displaying images with a small number of colors. JPEG images are not supported natively by all browsers, but they have smaller file sizes and look better when displaying images that have a lot of colors. If Grace uses the GIF format, she's assured that the images will look good and can be displayed by all Web browsers.

Use inline images

A graphic image can be inserted into an HTML document as an inline image. An inline image displays in a Web page, as shown in Figure 3-1; requires no helper programs and doesn't have to be downloaded to be viewed; and can be aligned with text using special HTML tags. Since inline images make your document look great, Grace wants to include several of them, including the Nomad logo.

Explanatory text following images

Although it's becoming a rarity, not all Web browsers can display images. For users of text-only browsers, Grace will occasionally include descriptive text following her inline images. This text is helpful to those without graphic browsers, and can add valuable explanations to displayed images.

Create links between images and Web sites

Just as clicking linked text in a Web page can take you to a different Web site, an image can also be linked to other sites. In addition to making an image "clickable," clicking specific areas of an inline image can take you to different Web locations. Linked images display in a Web page surrounded by a dark border, as shown in Figure 3-1.

FIGURE 3-1: Inline and linked images make a Web page look professional

Inline graphic image

Dark border
surrounds linked
image

Pointer changes in
linked image

TABLE 3-1: Common graphic file formats

FORMAT	EXTENSION	SUPPORT PROVIDED
Graphics Interchange Format	GIF	Native
Joint Photographic Experts Group	JPEG, JPG	Native
PC Paintbrush	PCX	External
Tagged Image File Format	TIFF	External
Windows Bitmap	BMP	External

TROUBLE?

If an image displays as
an icon, the image's
file format is not
natively supported by
your browser, or you
have not typed the
HTML tags
correctly.■

Using inline graphics

An inline graphic image is easy to add to an HTML document. The HTML image tag is <IMG SRC=*"image_location"*>; it is an empty container, so it does not require a closing tag. Once this tag is in the document, additional codes can be used to affect the size, position, and alignment of the graphic image on the page. Commonly used codes, or **attributes**, are defined in Table 3-2. **case** Grace has a graphics file containing the Nomad Ltd logo that she wants to add to her Web page.

1 Start WordPad, open the file HTML 3-1.htm, then save it as Nomad Home Page.htm on your Student Disk
Grace has inserted several text placeholders in the document to help her position graphic images correctly.

2 Select the **INSERT INLINE GRAPHIC HERE** placeholder
A graphic file is inserted into a Web document by using the image tag, IMG, and the attribute that defines the source, SRC. The information is typed into an empty container; there is no ending tag. An inline graphic image is automatically left-aligned when it's inserted into a document unless you specify otherwise. Grace wants her image to be right-aligned on the page.

3 Type **<IMG SRC="file:///a1/nomad.gif" ALIGN="right">**, then press **[Enter]**, as shown in Figure 3-2   ⤷ Case Sensitive
The ALIGN attribute lets you position an image on a page, as well as where text on the same line appears. The LEFT and RIGHT options let you specify the margin alignment of the image; the TOP, MIDDLE, and BOTTOM options let you specify where the image will display relative to text on the same line.

The HTML code is in the document and Grace saves her work.

4 Click the **Save button** 🖫 on the toolbar
Next, Grace starts Netscape Navigator and views the document.

5 Start Netscape Navigator and open the Nomad Home Page.htm file
Compare your Web page with Figure 3-3. Continue to the next lesson.

TABLE 3-2: Common IMG attributes

HTML ATTRIBUTE	DESCRIPTION	STATUS
ALIGN	Physically aligns image on the page	Optional
ALT	Specifies alternative text a user can also click	Optional
ISMAP	Specifies that image is an image map	Optional
SRC	Specifies an image source or location	Necessary

FIGURE 3-2: Inline image container with alignment attribute

Affect image positon using ALIGN

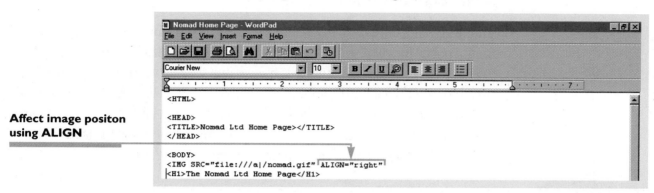

FIGURE 3-3: Right-aligned inline image

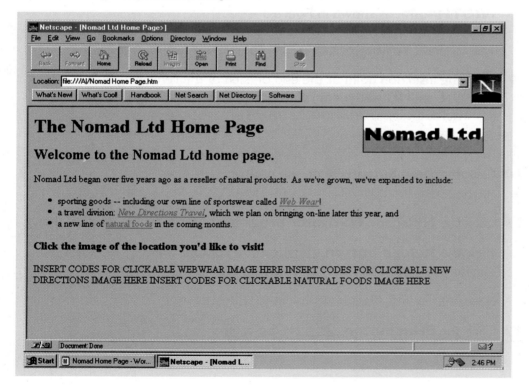

QUICK **TIP**

The ALIGN attribute can be typed before or after the SRC code in the IMG container. ▶ ALIGN attributes may be typed in upper- or lowercase.■

TROUBLE?

Confused about the strange HTML symbols used to reference files? See the related topic "Translating DOS symbols to HTML" in Unit 1.■

Using inline graphics, continued

Inline graphics are easy to insert into a Web document, but unfortunately, they might not be the right size. Using the additional ALIGN attributes HEIGHT and WIDTH, you can make your graphic images any size you want. ▶ Since some Web browsers do not have graphics capabilities, you can offer readers a "text only" option. See the related topic "Offering a 'text only' option" for more information. ▶**case** Grace wants to display a small graphic image for each of the items in her unordered list at the end of each line so they are the same size.

6 Click the **WordPad program button** on the taskbar
The Nomad Home Page document displays. You use the IMG container, with the added attributes of HEIGHT and WIDTH, to size a graphic image. Grace wants each image to be the same height.

7 Place the insertion point at the end of the Web Wear bulleted line, then press **[Enter]**
Grace types the IMG container.

8 Type **<IMG SRC="file:///a|/webwear.gif" HEIGHT=35 WIDTH=60>**, as shown in Figure 3-4
Grace would like to add graphic images to the remaining bulleted lines. The logo for New Directions Travel is compass.gif; the logo for the natural foods line is food.gif.

9 Place the insertion point at the end of each of the remaining bulleted lines, then type an IMG statement referencing the graphic image for that file
Your WordPad document should look like Figure 3-4.

Now that the IMG containers are written, Grace saves her work.

10 Click the **Save button** 🖫 on the toolbar
Next Grace views her document in Netscape Navigator.

11 Click the **Netscape Navigator program button** on the taskbar, then click the **Reload button** 🔄 on the toolbar
Compare your Netscape Navigator page with Figure 3-5.

Pleased with her work, Grace decides to print her Web page.

12 Click the **Print button** 🖨 on the toolbar

FIGURE 3-4: Graphic images with HEIGHT and WIDTH attributes

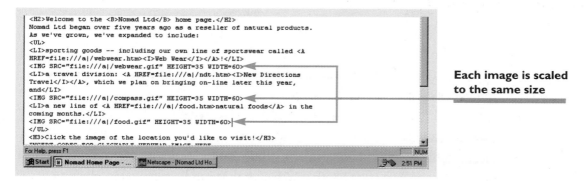

```
<H2>Welcome to the <B>Nomad Ltd</B> home page.</H2>
Nomad Ltd began over five years ago as a reseller of natural products.
As we've grown, we've expanded to include:
<UL>
<LI>sporting goods -- including our own line of sportswear called <A
HREF=file:///a|/webwear.htm><I>Web Wear</I></A>!</LI>
<IMG SRC="file:///a|/webwear.gif" HEIGHT=35 WIDTH=60>
<LI>a travel division: <A HREF=file:///a|/ndt.htm><I>New Directions
Travel</I></A>, which we plan on bringing on-line later this year,
and</LI>
<IMG SRC="file:///a|/compass.gif" HEIGHT=35 WIDTH=60>
<LI>a new line of <A HREF=file:///a|/food.htm>natural foods</A> in the
coming months.</LI>
<IMG SRC="file:///a|/food.gif" HEIGHT=35 WIDTH=60>
</UL>
<H3>Click the image of the location you'd like to visit!</H3>
```

Each image is scaled to the same size

FIGURE 3-5: Scaled inline images

Spacing between lines in a list changes when images are added

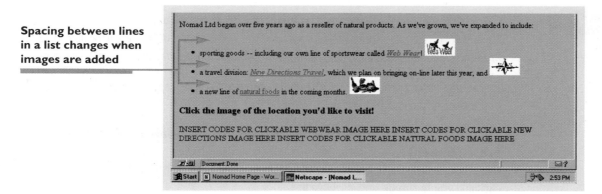

Offering a "text only" option

Since some Web browsers cannot display graphic images due to software or hardware limitations, you can include a "text only" option in a Web page containing graphic images. For example, the following statement: "Click <A HREF="file:///al/plain.htm">here</A> for a "text only" version of this page" can be added to your HTML document. The file plain.htm is the same HTML document with the graphic images deleted. This makes your Web page more meaningful to those users who cannot view graphic images.

Link to an HTML document with no graphics

FIGURE 3-6: A "text only" statement in a Web page

QUICK **TIP**

HEIGHT and WIDTH attributes are measured in pixels and are relative to the actual dimensions of the original image. They force an image to be scaled to new dimensions.■

Linking graphics

You've already learned how to link one Web page to another by clicking text. You've also learned how to insert a graphic image on a Web page. So, doesn't it make sense to be able to link one Web page to another by clicking a graphic image? Of course. In fact, the same HTML tag you used to create the text link <A HREF="*location*"> can be combined with the <IMG SRC="*location*"> tag. You can also include additional text with a graphic image so Web users who lack graphic capabilities can view the link. ▶case   Grace wants to create links on the Nomad Web page to other Web sites that can be accessed by clicking a graphic image or text.

1 Click the **WordPad program button** on the taskbar
Since Nomad's customers are health conscious, Grace wants readers of her page to be able to jump to a fitness Web site called the Health & Fitness World Guide Forum by clicking a graphic image.

2 Place the insertion point to the right of the **</UL>** tag, then press **[Enter]**
Grace wants to create a heading for this link.

3 Type **<H3>Want information on becoming healthier?</H3>**, then press **[Enter]**
Next, Grace sets up the link to the Health & Fitness World Guide Forum Web site by creating a clickable graphic image and clickable text.

4 Type **Check out the <A HREF="http://www.worldguide.com/Fitness/hf.html"><IMG SRC="file:///a | /fitness.gif"> Health & Fitness World Guide Forum</A> Web site**
Grace wants to align the text on this line with the top of the image, so she adds the ALIGN attribute to the IMG container. She also wants the image to be much smaller than its original size.

5 Place the insertion point after "file:///a | /fitness.gif", press **[Spacebar]**, then type **ALIGN="top" HEIGHT=60 WIDTH=30**
Compare your work with Figure 3-7.

Grace is ready to save her work and view the Web page.

6 Click the **Save button** 🖫 on the toolbar, then click the **Netscape Navigator program button** on the taskbar
Since changes have been made in the WordPad document, Grace reloads it in Netscape Navigator.

7 Click the **Reload button** on the toolbar
The Web page displays, as shown in Figure 3-8. Notice that the image is surrounded by a blue outline which indicates that the image is linked. By clicking either the image or the text following it, the reader jumps to the linked Web site.

FIGURE 3-7: HTML tags for linked image

Link to Web site

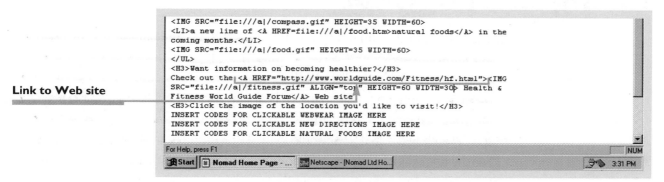

```
<IMG SRC="file:///a|/compass.gif" HEIGHT=35 WIDTH=60>
<LI>a new line of <A HREF=file:///a|/food.htm>natural foods</A> in the
coming months.</LI>
<IMG SRC="file:///a|/food.gif" HEIGHT=35 WIDTH=60>
</UL>
<H3>Want information on becoming healthier?</H3>
Check out the <A HREF="http://www.worldguide.com/Fitness/hf.html"><IMG
SRC="file:///a|/fitness.gif" ALIGN="top" HEIGHT=60 WIDTH=30> Health &
Fitness World Guide Forum</A> Web site
<H3>Click the image of the location you'd like to visit!</H3>
INSERT CODES FOR CLICKABLE WEBWEAR IMAGE HERE
INSERT CODES FOR CLICKABLE NEW DIRECTIONS IMAGE HERE
INSERT CODES FOR CLICKABLE NATURAL FOODS IMAGE HERE
```

FIGURE 3-8: Linked image and text

Click text or image to jump to link

Link displays in status line

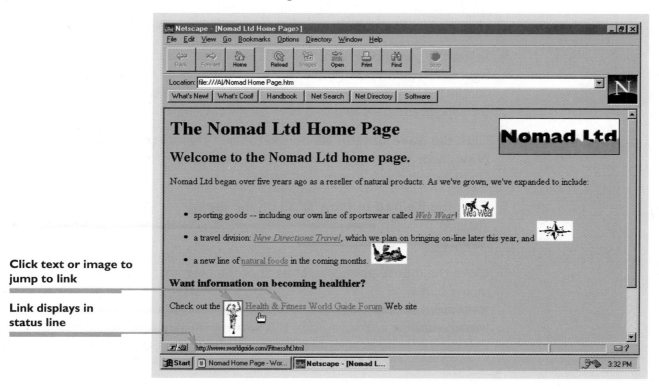

Creating image maps

The instinct to click an image is natural; clicking different areas within an image can jump you to different Web sites. You can set up a single graphics file as an **image map** "button" that will jump the reader to another Web site when it is clicked. Creating an image map can be tricky; each clickable area, or **hot spot**, within an image must be identified using pixel coordinates. You can set the hot spot by adding the ISMAP attribute to the IMG container in your HTML document. See the related topic "How pixel coordinates work" for more information. ▶ **ase** Grace wants to create image maps that will jump readers to different Web sites. She'll use her browser to determine the pixel coordinates before creating the images to click.

1 Click the **WordPad program button** on the taskbar
   Grace needs to determine the pixel coordinates that will jump readers to other Web sites.

2 Select the **INSERT CODES FOR CLICKABLE WEB WEAR IMAGE HERE** placeholder, then type **<A HREF="file:///a1/Nomad image.map"><IMG SRC="file:///a1/webwear.gif" HEIGHT=100 ISMAP></A>**, then press **[Enter]**
   The pixel coordinates for all the images in this page will be stored in a separate file called Nomad image.map. Grace will create that file once she's determined all the coordinates.

3 Select the placeholders for the IMG tags, type the tags shown in Figure 3-9, then press **[Enter]**
   Once the tags are typed, Grace saves her work and views the document in Netscape Navigator to determine the pixel coordinates to be stored in the Nomad image.map file.

4 Click the **Save button** 💾 on the toolbar, then click the **Netscape Navigator program button** on the taskbar
   Grace reloads the image to see the latest changes.

5 Click the **Reload button** 🔄 on the toolbar
   The image is updated. Grace will use her mouse pointer to determine the pixel coordinates she'll reference in her image map document.

6 Move the mouse pointer over each of the new images, *but don't click the mouse button*
   Notice that as the pointer moves over an image, its pixel coordinates are displayed in the browser's status bar, as shown in Figure 3-10. Grace notes the pixel coordinates at the center of each image so she can create the Nomad image.map file. Continue to the next lesson.

FIGURE 3-9: Completed IMG tags

Additional image map tags

FIGURE 3-10: Determining pixel coordinates in Netscape Navigator

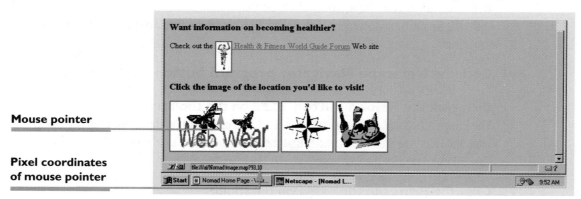

Mouse pointer

Pixel coordinates of mouse pointer

How pixel coordinates work

When a point in an image is clicked, the closest referenced point in the image map is activated. Since the likelihood that a reader will click the exact coordinates you specified in your image map document is low, it is important to choose the coordinates carefully. Make sure multiple points are not too close to one another, or your reader might accidentally jump to the wrong Web site.

TROUBLE?

Clicking an unavailable or fictitious Web site gives no results.■

Creating image maps, continued

Pixel coordinates are stored in a separate WordPad document that identifies which Web site the reader will jump to when the image is clicked. In an on-line Web session, clicking an image map connects you to the site identified in the image map document. When not on-line, clicking an image map results in the pointer changing to an hourglass while your computer searches for the site. You can also create an e-mail link so readers can send mail directly to the page administrator. See the related topic "Using the ADDRESS tags" for more information. ▶**ase**   Grace creates the image map document that contains the pixel coordinates to other Web sites that she will insert later.

7 Click the **WordPad program button** on the taskbar

8 Click the **New button** 🔲 on the toolbar, click **Text Document** in the New dialog box, then click **OK**
Grace determined a single point in each image that she'll link to Web sites that she'll insert later. In addition to the pixel coordinates, she'll include comment lines to identify the sites by name. Each comment line begins with the pound sign (#). Grace types placeholders for the real Web sites.

9 Type the information in Figure 3-11
Now that Grace has typed the coordinates, she saves the document.

10 Click the **Save button** 💾 on the toolbar, type **Nomad image.map** in the File name text box, then click **Save**
Once the image map document is complete, Grace refreshes the Web page that contains the images.

11 Click the **Netscape Navigator program button** on the taskbar,

then click the **Reload button** [Reload] on the toolbar
The image is updated, as shown in Figure 3-12. She can return to the image map document later and insert the Web site locations that the reader will jump to when each image is clicked. Grace decides to print the Web page.

12 Click the **Print button** [Print] on the toolbar

FIGURE 3-11:
Image map document
with pixel coordinates

 # indicates comment
line

Pixel coordinates

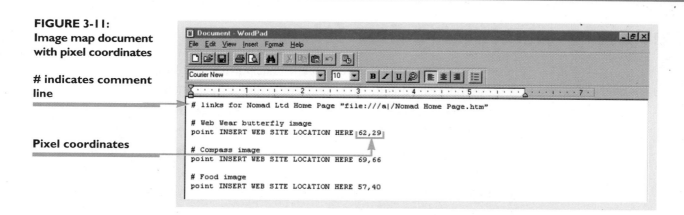

FIGURE 3-12:
Completed image map
graphic images

All images have the
same height

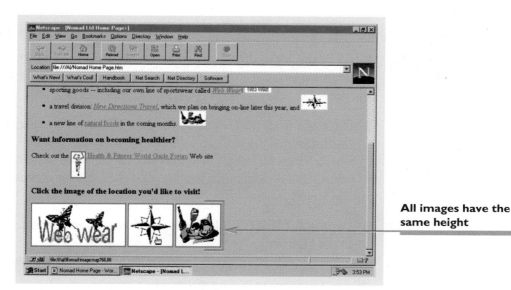

Using the ADDRESS tags

Make it easy for your readers to contact you by including your postal address and/or e-mail address within the ADDRESS tags. The information in these tags displays in italics. If your readers are using Netscape Navigator, you can include the MAILTO attribute to allow your readers to send e-mail to you with a single mouse click. The statement <A HREF="MAILTO:Gdekmejian@nomadltd.com"> GDekmejian@nomadltd.com</A> results in the link, as shown in Figure 3-13.

Click to create e-mail

Result of <ADDRESS>
</ADDRESS> tags

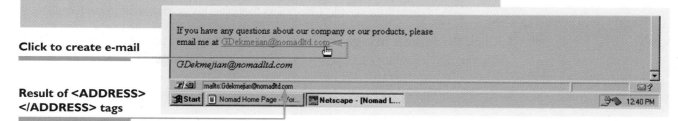

FIGURE 3-13: The MAILTO attribute in a link

Inserting multimedia files

Most computers used today are capable of displaying beautiful images and videos with sound. Full-motion videos and sound files are commonly referred to as **multimedia**. Full-motion videos tend to have larger file sizes that make them cumbersome on the Internet. Audio files have varying sizes, are simple to use, and can be heard through a standard computer speaker. To see or hear multimedia files on your computer, you need to configure your browser to work with **helper programs**, which are independent programs that let you use multimedia files. See the related topic "Using helper programs" for more information. ▶**case** Grace wants to add an audio file to her Web page to take advantage of the Web's multimedia capabilities.

1 Click the **WordPad program button** on the taskbar
Grace decides to add an audio file at the end of the "Welcome to the Nomad Ltd home page" heading.

2 Place the insertion point to the left of the </H2> tag, then press **[Enter]**
Inserting a multimedia file requires two HTML tags: the <A HREF></A> tag identifies the location of the audio file, and the <IMG SRC> tag allows the reader to see or hear the file. Grace begins by defining the location of the audio file; she'll use sound files that come with Windows 95.

3 Type **<A HREF="file:///c | /windows/media/tada.wav">**, then press **[Enter]**
Next, she enters the location of the image the reader will click to hear the sound.

4 Type **<IMG SRC="file:///a | /sound.gif"></A>**
Compare your document with Figure 3-14. Grace is ready to hear the audio file in the Web page, so she saves her work.

5 Click the **Save button** 🖫 on the toolbar
Next, Grace switches to Netscape Navigator and reloads the WordPad document.

6 Click the **Netscape Navigator program button** on the taskbar, then click the **Reload button** 🔄 on the toolbar
The document displays with a linked image following the Welcome heading, as shown in Figure 3-15. To hear the audio file, Grace clicks the linked image to start the helper program.

7 Click the **linked image** 🖼 then click the **Play button** ▶ on the toolbar
Satisfied with her work, Grace closes Netscape Navigator and WordPad.

8 Close Netscape Navigator and WordPad

FIGURE 3-14: HTML tags for a multimedia file

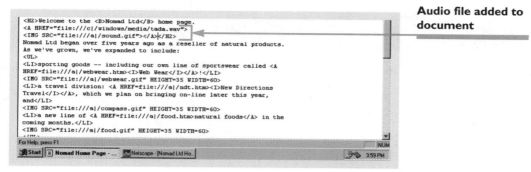

Audio file added to document

FIGURE 3-15: Inline image linked to an audio file

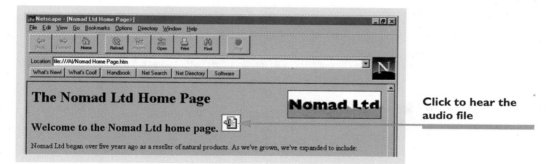

Click to hear the audio file

Using helper programs

Helper programs allow your computer to play multimedia files. Media Player is a helper program that comes with Windows 95; others can be purchased commercially or downloaded from the Internet. You must install and configure the helper program before using it. In Netscape Navigator, click Options on the menu bar, click General Preferences, then click the Helpers tab. Scroll down until the file extension you want to configure displays, click the Launch the Application radio button, locate the program file, then click OK. Figure 3-16 shows the Media Player configured for .wav multimedia files.

Helper program displays here

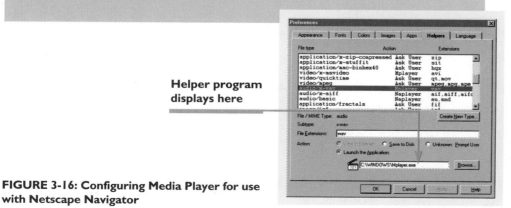

FIGURE 3-16: Configuring Media Player for use with Netscape Navigator

TROUBLE?

No Windows folder? Ask your instructor or technical support person for assistance.■

TASKREFERENCE

TASK	KEYBOARD
Add italicized address	Type <ADDRESS>*text*</ADDRESS>
Change inline image alignment	Type ALIGN="left," "right," "top," "middle," or "bottom" within IMG tag
Configure a helper program	(in Netscape Navigator) Click Options, General Preferences
Create a clickable image map	Type ISMAP attribute within the <IMG SRC> tag
Create an image map document	Type pixel coordinates in a text document
Create comment lines in an image map document	Begin line with pound sign (#)
Create e-mail statement	Type MAILTO attribute within <A HREF> tag
Create "text only" option	Type <A HREF="*file_location*"></A> tag referencing a plain HTML file
Determine pixel coordinates	Determine coordinates from a Web browser
Insert inline image	Type <IMG SRC="*image_location*">
Insert multimedia	Type <A HREF="*file_location*"> <IMG SRC="*file_location*"></A>
Link a graphic image	Type <A HREF> tag followed by a <IMG SRC></A> tag
Scale inline image	Type HEIGHT=*size* and/or WIDTH=*size* within IMG tag

CONCEPTSREVIEW

Label each element of the Netscape Navigator screen shown in Figure 3-17.

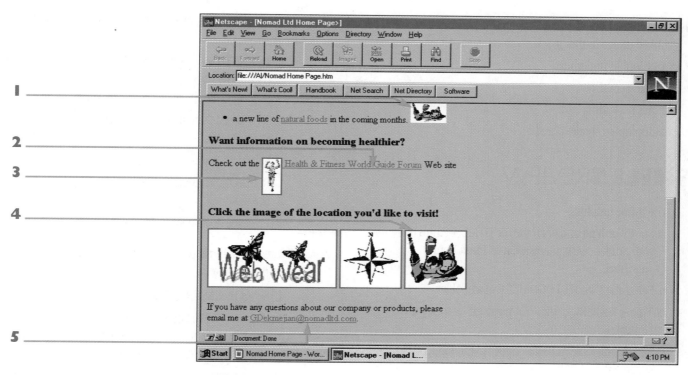

FIGURE 3-17

Match each statement with the HTML attributes it describes.

6 Italicizes address

7 Adds text to image

8 Indicates image map

9 Indicates image source

10 Determines text/margin position

a. ALIGN

b. ADDRESS

c. SRC

d. ISMAP

e. ALT

Select the best answer from the list of choices.

11 Which is not a common Internet graphics file format?

a. AUZ

b. GIF

c. TIFF

d. BMP

12 You can identify image map locations by using

a. helper programs

b. addressable images

c. pixel coordinates

d. local access points

1 3 All of the following are attributes of ALIGN, *except*

    a. top

    b. right

    c. bottom

    d. under

1 4 The appearance of a linked image differs from a non-linked image in that it

    a. is double-underlined

    b. has an outline

    c. has no outline

    d. displays in shades of red

SKILLSREVIEW

1 Use inline graphics.

    a. Start WordPad and open the file HTML 3-2.htm on your Student Disk, then save it as Pizza home page.htm.

    b. Select the INSERT LOGO HERE placeholder.

    c. Type <IMG SRC="file:///al/pizza.gif"> then press [Enter].

    d. Add the attribute ALIGN="right" to the IMG statement.

    e. Save your work.

    f. View your work in Netscape Navigator, then return to WordPad.

    g. Select the INSERT SMALL LOGO HERE placeholder.

    h. Insert the pizza.gif file using Height=40 and Width=50 attributes.

    i. Select the INSERT IMAGE #1 HERE placeholder, and insert the stress.gif file from your Student Disk using a height and width of 40.

    j. Select the INSERT IMAGE #2 HERE placeholder and insert the pressure.gif file from your Student Disk using a height and width of 40.

    k. Save your work.

    l. View the document in Netscape Navigator.

    m. Print the document in Netscape Navigator.

2 Link graphics.

    a. Return to WordPad.

    b. Select the INSERT LINKED GRAPHIC HERE placeholder.

    c. Type an HTML tag that creates a link to the (fictitious) Web site http://www.istellar.pizza.com/faqs.htm.

    d. Type an IMG tag that links to pizza.gif on your Student Disk.

    e. Save your work.

    f. Reload the changes to the document in Netscape Navigator.

    g. Print the document in Netscape Navigator.

3 Create image maps.

    a. Return to WordPad.

    b. Select the INSERT IMAGE #3 HERE placeholder.

    c. Write an HTML tag referencing the image map file Pizza image.map (to be created later) that links the pixel coordinates of the four buttons in menu.gif.

    d. Use Netscape Navigator—or your browser—to determine pixel coordinates for each of the four buttons at the bottom of the graphic image.

    e. Write down the four pixel coordinates.

    f. Open a new WordPad document and save it as a text document called Pizza image.map on your Student Disk.

    g. Create four statements: one that points to each set of pixel coordinates, then save your work. Assume that clicking each button jumps the reader to a Web site (using the fictitious site http://www.istellar.pizza.com/) where you make up the name of each file. (For example, the Web site for the first button on the left could be called http://www.istellar.pizza.com/Safety.htm.)

h. Save your work.

i. Print the document in WordPad.

j. Reload the changes to the Pizza Home Page document in Netscape Navigator. (*Note:* Clicking any of the buttons in the image will result in an error message, since you have created fictitious Web sites.)

k. Print the document in Netscape Navigator.

finish
skip
4 Insert a multimedia file.

a. Return to WordPad.

b. Place the insertion point after "Allow one light year for delivery!".

c. Type an HTML tag that links the chimes.wav audio file (located in the c:\windows\media\ folder).

d. Type an IMG tag that links the multimedia file to sound.gif on your Student Disk.

e. Save your work.

f. Print the WordPad document.

g. Reload the changes to the document in Netscape Navigator.

h. Play the sound image.

i. Close Media Player when the sound is finished.

j. Print the document in Netscape Navigator.

k. Close and exit Netscape Navigator and WordPad.

l. Submit your printed materials.

INDEPENDENT
CHALLENGE 1

5/7/99   Done

You'd like to incorporate the Star Dot Star consulting firm's logo into its Web page and to use other graphic images to make your pages more effective and attractive. You've already created the logo and have other graphics files, now you'll insert these files and create links to other sites.

To complete this independent challenge:

1 Open the file Star Dot Star-page 1.htm in WordPad that you created in Unit 2, then save it as Star Dot Star - home page.htm.

2 Insert the logo file, stardot.gif, in a prominent location on the page.

3 Insert the same file in an additional location, but scaled to a smaller size.

4 Create a link to the (fictitious) Web site http://www.hi-tech.com using a graphic image of your choice, as well as text.

5 Create a text-only text link to your page.

6 Add one additional inline image (from any available source) to the page.

7 Print the document in WordPad.

8 Print the document in Netscape Navigator.

9 Submit your printed materials.

INDEPENDENT
CHALLENGE 2

The Board of Realtors loves your work so much they've created a new logo for you to incorporate into their Web site. Realtors know that presentation is very important, so they've asked you to jazz up their Web pages with graphic images, links, and sounds.

To complete this independent challenge:

1 Open the file you created in Unit 2 called Real Estate.htm and save it as Realtors Home Page.htm.

2 Make any necessary modifications to the text as you see fit.

3 Insert the Board of Realtors logo file, realtors.gif, on your Student Disk somewhere towards the top of this page.

4 Find a (real) Web site that prospective home buyers might find interesting, and create a link to it.

5 Add at least two sounds to your page using the .wav files provided in the c:\windows\media folder on your hard drive or server.

6 Use the sound.gif file as a link to the sounds.

7 Insert a smaller version of realtors.gif elsewhere on the page.

8 Save your work.

9 Print the document in WordPad.

10 Print the document in Netscape Navigator.

11 Submit your printed materials.

INDEPENDENT
CHALLENGE 3

The reaction to your in-store information system at Film Clips is very encouraging. In fact, you've decided to enhance your Web pages by adding sounds and graphic images. Many images are available on the Web, and here's your opportunity to do some quality surfing. You've also designed a logo and have that in electronic form. Film Clips specializes in your favorite kind of movies.

To complete this independent challenge:

1 Create an outline for an explanatory page about a retrospective about your favorite movie star.

2 Open a blank WordPad document, and save it as a text document called Film Clips Home Page.htm on your Student Disk.

3 Type the outline in the document, using the appropriate HTML tags.

4 Insert the logo, filmclip.gif, located on your Student Disk. Use any alignment for the logo you feel is appropriate.

5 Surf the Web to find at least one graphic image of your movie star, then download it.

6 Include this graphic image on your page.

7 Locate a real Web site containing information on this movie star, then create a link so your customers can click the image in Step 6 to jump to this Web site.

8 Save your work.

9 Print the document in WordPad.

10 Print the document in Netscape Navigator.

11 Submit your printed materials.

INDEPENDENT
CHALLENGE 4

Madam Zylog, your client, is determined to be the foremost astrologer, fortune teller, and palm reader on the World Wide Web. She's pleased with your work so far, but has had a vision of many graphic images. Madam Zylog feels strongly that you are the one to provide these images.

To complete this independent challenge:

1 Create an outline for a new Web page that will concentrate on Madam Zylog's talents.

2 Open a new WordPad document, and save it as a text document called Madam Zylog Home Page 1.htm on your Student Disk.

3 Insert her logo, zylog.gif, on your Student Disk.

4 Insert a sound on the page using a scaled version of her logo as the clickable image that starts the helper program.

5 Locate a real Web site about each of Madam Zylog's talents.

6 Download a new graphic image (or use her logo) and determine three pixel coordinates using your Web browser.

7 Create an image map that connects to each of these Web sites in a new WordPad text document called Madam Zylog.map.

8 Save your work.

9 Print the WordPad and Netscape Navigator documents.

10 Submit your printed materials.

VISUAL WORKSHOP

Use the skills you learned in this unit to create the Web page shown in Figure 3-18. Save the HTML file on your Student Disk in WordPad as a text document called Barbara's Home Page.htm, then print the document in WordPad and Netscape Navigator. Use the graphics files barbaras.gif and cookie.gif on your Student Disk; use the fictitious Web site http://www.barbaras.com/recipes.htm.

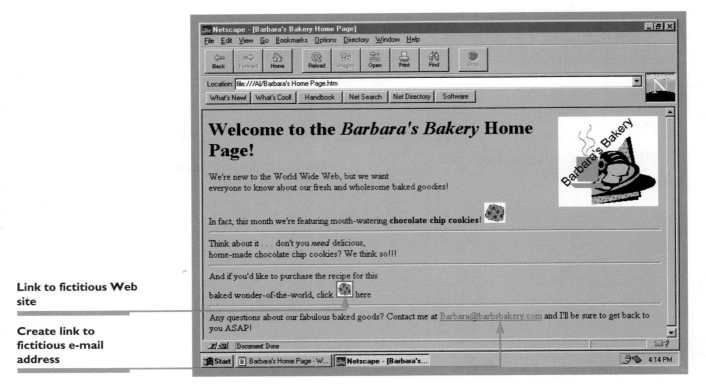

Link to fictitious Web site

Create link to fictitious e-mail address

FIGURE 3-18: Barbara's Bakery Home Page

UNIT 4

OBJECTIVES

▶ Plan a form

▶ Create a text entry field

▶ Use checkboxes and radio buttons

▶ Use pull-down menus and scroll boxes

▶ Use push buttons with preset values

Using
FORMS TO CONTROL INPUT

Businesses using the World Wide Web to introduce customers to their products can also use their Web pages to take customer's orders. HTML has a variety of tags that can be used to create helpful forms that easily accept user input. ◆ase The purpose of Nomad's Web pages is not only to introduce its products to a wider audience, but also to make on-line purchases simple. Grace wants to include a form that makes it easy for customers to make purchases. ▶

Planning a Form

A form is a great way of gathering information for later use. For a business that uses the Web, a form is a great way of collecting information about customer preferences and taking orders. A Web page form can accept input by allowing a user to type text or click radio buttons, checkboxes, or labeled buttons to make selections. Table 4-1 lists the three HTML tags that are used to create these items on a form. See the related topic "Printing a Web page" for information needed to print your Web pages in these lessons. **case** Grace decides what types of fields she wants in the Nomad order form:

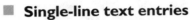

▎ **Single-line text entries**
A user can simply type entries in a text box, much like on a paper form. When the text box is defined, you can set its maximum length to ensure a professional look. Grace will use a text box for the customer to enter his/her name.

▎ **Checkboxes and radio buttons**
Many forms are simplified by allowing a user to make selections and a Web page is no exception. Choices are commonly made in the form of checkboxes and radio buttons, as shown in Figure 4-1. Frequently, the user is asked to choose one item from a list (although it is possible to make multiple selections using special tags). In addition to giving the user a list of choices, you can also supply a default selection—an item that is automatically selected—to make filling out the form that much quicker.

▎ **Pull-down menus and scroll boxes**
To avoid cluttering a form with lengthy lists, a more attractive option can be a scroll box or pull-down menu. Each of these selection methods can also display an automatic default value. For items with several options, Grace will use a pull-down menu.

▎ **Multi-line text areas**
Even though a form should require as little typing as possible for the user, it's nice to offer customers the option of commenting without restriction. Grace wants to include an area in which a customer can freely comment on Nomad and its products.

▎ **Push buttons with preset functions**
Once a customer makes selections on the order form, the information must be sent to an order desk where it is processed for delivery and billing. Grace wants to design a single button that a customer clicks when the order form is finished to send the information.

FIGURE 4-1: Sample order form for user input

Click radio button to make a selection

User types text entry here

Pull-down menu with default selection

Checkbox options with a default already selected

Look Here

Printing a Web page

To print a Web page so it displays elements such as checkboxes and radio buttons, you must take a "picture" of what is on your screen by pressing the Print Screen button on your keyboard; this places an image of your screen on the computer's Clipboard. Then you can start the Paint or Paintbrush program, which comes with Windows, click Edit on the menu bar, then click Paste. To fit the image on a single sheet of paper, change the paper orientation to landscape by clicking File on the menu bar, then clicking Page Setup. To print the image, click File on the menu bar, then click Print.

TROUBLE?

Can't find the Print Screen button on your keyboard? There are many variations of this key. It might appear as "Print Scrn" or "PrtSc," depending on the type of keyboard you have. It is usually located to the right of the F12 key.■

TABLE 4-1: HTML field creation tags

TAG	RESULT
INPUT	Creates a variety of fields: single text lines, radio buttons, checkboxes, and push buttons
SELECT	Creates a field in which a user makes choices from a scroll box or pull-down menu
TEXTAREA	Creates a field that accepts multiple lines of user text

Creating a text entry field

A single line of text is the simplest entry to create on a form. A text entry field is created using the INPUT TYPE tags. Other INPUT tags are listed in Table 4-2. Regardless of the type of field, each form begins and ends with the <FORM> </FORM> tags. Each <FORM> tag must also indicate how the information on the form is transmitted. The initial <FORM> tag is used in combination with either the ACTION or METHOD tag in order to correctly send the completed form.

▶ **case**   Grace started her document and left spaces to fill in necessary information. She begins by adding a field for a customer to enter his/her name.

1   **Start WordPad, then open the file HTML 4-1.htm and save it as Nomad on-line order form.htm on your Student Disk**
The first HTML tag necessary when creating a form field is the <FORM> tag. This tag must be accompanied by the tags ACTION or METHOD, so the information is properly sent.

2   **Place the insertion point in the blank line under the <HR>, then type <FORM ACTION="URL">**
By including the ACTION tag in this statement, Grace can send the information in the form to a URL location (which she'll supply later to replace the URL placeholder).

3   **Type Please tell us your name:, then press [Enter]**
Next, Grace defines the type, size, and name of the text field. Text fields are created using the INPUT TEXT tag. Grace will use additional tags to define the field's size and name.

4   **Type <INPUT TYPE="TEXT" SIZE=20 NAME="yourname">, then press [Enter]**
Grace ends the form with the final FORM tag.

5   **Type </FORM>**
Compare your document with Figure 4-2.

Now Grace saves her work and sees how the text field looks.

6   **Click the Save button 🔲 on the toolbar**
Grace starts Netscape Navigator and views the document.

7   **Start Netscape Navigator and open the file Nomad on-line order form.htm from your Student Disk**
Compare your Web page with Figure 4-3.

Continue to the next lesson.

underconstruction 98
ZDnet.com
search by name
and HTML

FIGURE 4-2:
HTML tags for
text field

only use 1 form action tag
at top and one end form
tag at the bottom.

Begins a form

Tag determines type
and size of field

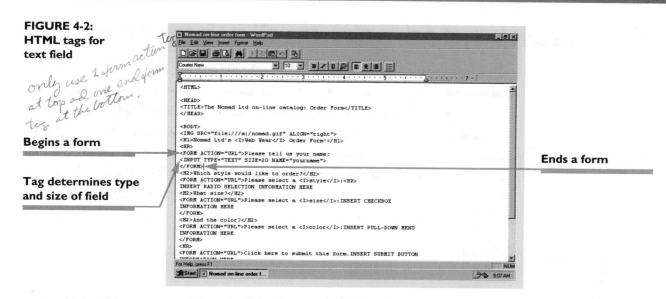

Ends a form

FIGURE 4-3:
Text field in form

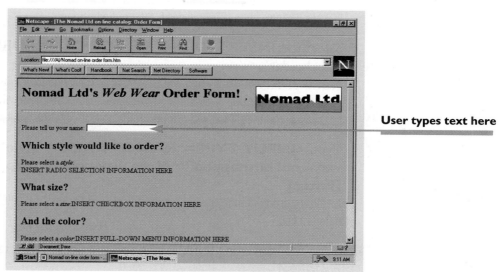

User types text here

TABLE 4-2: HTML INPUT tags

INPUT TAG	DESCRIPTION
NAME	Defines the name of the data; a required field
SIZE	Determines the size of the field; measured in characters
MAXLENGTH	Determines the maximum number of allowable characters
VALUE	Defines the default value to be displayed
CHECKED	Determines which radio button or checkbox value is selected; works only with these two INPUT type tags
TYPE	Sets the input field to "text," "password," "radio," "checkbox," "reset," or "submit"

QUICK TIP

Try to eliminate clutter on a form; include only what's necessary or your page will look messy.

Using checkboxes and radio buttons

Making selections on a form should be as simple and error-free as possible. Using radio buttons and checkboxes in a form is one way of assuring easy and accurate data entry. Both radio buttons and checkboxes use the INPUT TYPE tags, but items in a list are grouped together by sharing a common NAME. Items displayed using checkboxes or radio buttons can be arranged using list tags or line breaks. See the related topic "Displaying radio buttons and checkboxes using a list format" for more information. ▶**ase** Grace uses radio buttons to allow customers to choose which style Web Wear T-shirt they want to order.

I Click the **WordPad program button** on the taskbar
The WordPad document appears.

Grace wants to add radio buttons to this form to make a customer's selection process easy. The FORM tags have already been typed for the radio buttons.

2 Select the **INSERT RADIO SELECTION INFORMATION HERE** placeholder
The INPUT TYPE for each entry will be "RADIO" as each item will have a radio button next to it. Each item in the group is given the NAME "style," and each item will have a unique VALUE. The text outside the INPUT tag will display on the page to help the reader make a choice.

← what gets sent

3 Type **<INPUT TYPE="RADIO" NAME="style" VALUE="Mega way-cool bitmapped">** **Mega way-cool bitmapped**, then press **[Enter]**
Each remaining item in the radio button list is similar, but has a different VALUE and different text.

4 Type the remaining INPUT tags and the final FORM tag, as shown in Figure 4-4.
Now that she's typed the INPUT tags, Grace saves her work.

5 Click the **Save button** 🖫 on the toolbar
Next, she views her document in Netscape Navigator.

6 Click the **Netscape Navigator program button** on the taskbar, then click the **Reload button** 🔄 on the toolbar
Compare your Netscape Navigator document with Figure 4-5.

Continue to the next lesson.

FIGURE 4-4:
INPUT tags for
radio button items

Input tags

Creates a radio
button display

Displays next to the
radio button

FIGURE 4-5:
Radio buttons in
HTML form

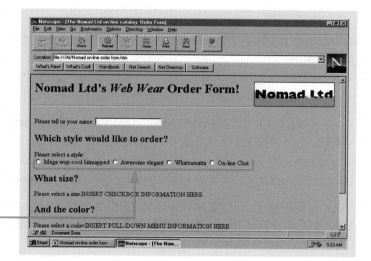

Radio buttons with no
default selection

using list format

Displaying radio buttons and checkboxes using a list format

Radio button and checkbox selections can be displayed horizontally (within a line of text, for example) or in a vertical list using ordered or definition list tags, or by inserting <BR> tags where you want each line to end. Definition tags (<DL> <DT> <DD>) can be used to create an indented effect, as shown in Figure 4-6.

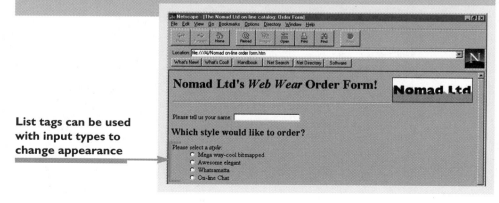

List tags can be used
with input types to
change appearance

FIGURE 4-6: Definition list tags create indented radio buttons

Using checkboxes and radio buttons, continued

Checkboxes are similar to radio buttons in that the user can make a selection from several items. When creating either checkboxes or radio buttons, you can select a default value—which automatically appears as selected—using the CHECKED tag. **ease** Grace wants to use a checkbox field so customers can select a size; she wants the default size, Medium, to be checked.

7 Click the **WordPad program button** on the taskbar
A placeholder marks the location of the HTML tags.

8 Select the **INSERT CHECKBOX INFORMATION HERE** placeholder
Since the FORM tags have already been typed, Grace can begin by typing the INPUT TYPE tags for the checkbox fields. The sizes available are small, medium, large, and x-large.

9 Type **<INPUT TYPE="CHECKBOX" NAME="sizes" VALUE="Small"> Small**, then press **[Enter]**
Next, she'll create the Medium checkbox; this item will be the default value. An item appears as checked (or on, for a radio button) by including the CHECKED tag in the INPUT statement.

10 Type **<INPUT TYPE="CHECKBOX" NAME="sizes" VALUE="Medium" CHECKED> Medium**, then press **[Enter]**
Grace completes the items in the checkbox list.

11 Type the remaining checkbox items, as shown in Figure 4-7
Grace is ready to save her work and view the Web page.

12 Click the **Save button** 🖫 on the toolbar, then click the **Netscape Navigator program button** on the taskbar
Grace needs to reload the document in Netscape Navigator.

13 Click the **Reload button** 🔃 on the toolbar
The Web page appears, as shown in Figure 4-8. The Medium checkbox automatically appears with a checkmark, as this is the default selection.

FIGURE 4-7: HTML tags for checkbox items

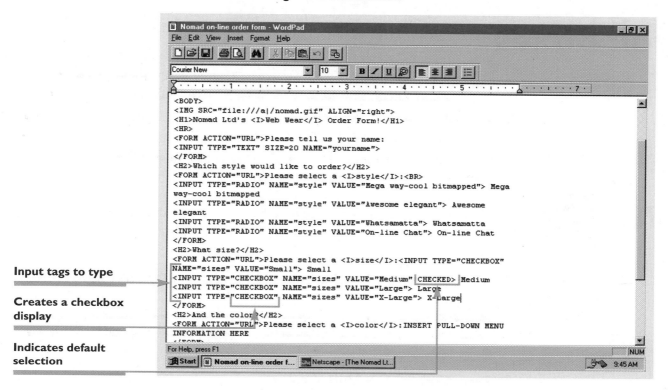

Input tags to type

Creates a checkbox display

Indicates default selection

FIGURE 4-8: Checkboxes on a Web page

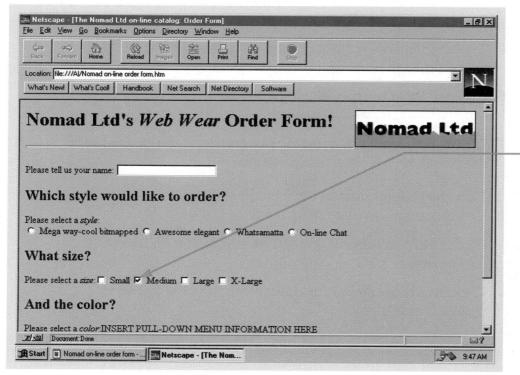

Default selection is automatically checked

TROUBLE?

When you first create checkboxes, some items might appear as checked when they shouldn't be. Reopening the file from the File menu correctly displays the checked items.∎

Using pull-down menus and scroll boxes

Depending on the layout of your Web page, you might want to offer choices to readers without displaying all the options on the page. Pull-down menus and scroll boxes use the SELECT tag; each of these display methods can be assigned a default value using the SELECTED tag. The SELECT tag has a variety of attributes that affect the appearance of the list. These attributes are described in Table 4-3. **ase** Grace wants to list the T-shirt color choices in a pull-down menu.

1 Click the **WordPad program button** on the taskbar
Grace will replace a placeholder in the document with the information needed for a simple pull-down menu.

2 Select the **INSERT PULL-DOWN MENU INFORMATION HERE** placeholder
A pull-down menu begins and ends with the initial <FORM ACTION> tag, but the closing </FORM> tag is not used. The SELECT tag defines the options in the list, and the first item in the list defines the name of the field. *add size=3 to make it a scroll window (or an number you want)*

3 Type **<SELECT NAME="color">**, then press **[Enter]**
Next, Grace types the first item in the list, which she wants as the default value. She'll include the SELECTED tag to indicate the default value.

4 Type **<OPTION SELECTED>Navy blue**, then press **[Enter]**
Now Grace types the remaining colors in the list and ends the list using the final SELECT tag.

5 Type the remaining colors and tags using Figure 4-9 as a guide
Since all the information is typed, Grace saves her work.

6 Click the **Save button** 🖫 on the toolbar
Next Grace switches to Netscape Navigator.

7 Click the **Netscape Navigator program button** on the taskbar
Grace reloads the document in Netscape Navigator.

8 Click the **Reload button** on the toolbar
The Web page appears, as shown in Figure 4-10.

Compare your document with Figure 4-10, using the scroll bar if necessary to see the pull-down menu.

9 Click the **arrow** on the pull-down menu to see all the items
Continue to the next lesson.

FIGURE 4-9:
Create a pull-down menu using the SELECT tags

Option tags to type

Determines the default selection

Creates a pull-down or scroll box display

Indicates the end of selection list

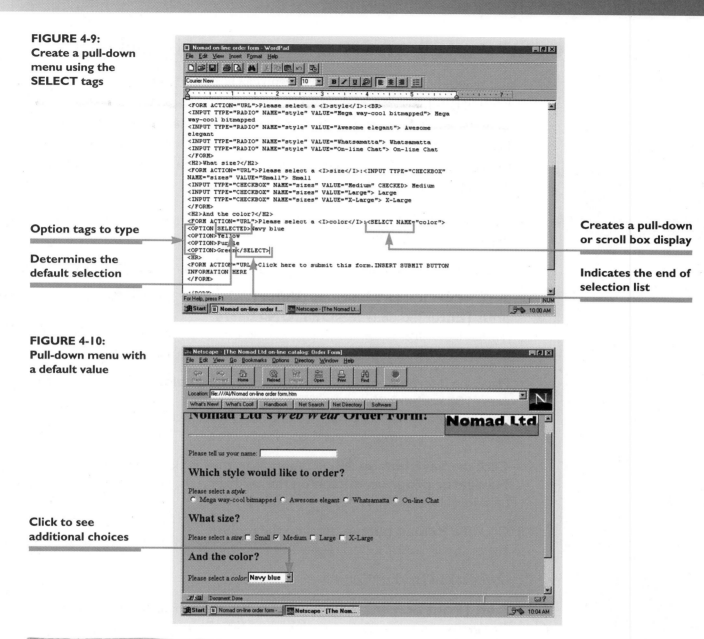

FIGURE 4-10:
Pull-down menu with a default value

Click to see additional choices

TABLE 4-3: SELECT tag attributes

SELECT TAG	DESCRIPTION
NAME	Defines the name of the data; a required field.
SIZE	Determines how many items display. If omitted, choices appear as pop-up menu; if set to 2 or more, appears as scroll box.
MULTIPLE	Allows more than one selection to be made; appears as a scroll box.
VALUE	The value to be assigned to a choice; an optional attribute that doesn't need to have the same value displayed on the page.
SELECTED	The choice to be the default option.

Using pull-down menus and scroll boxes, continued

You've seen how a simple pull-down menu can be created using the SELECT tags. Existing HTML tags can be modified to change a pull-down menu into a scroll box by adding the optional SIZE attribute to the SELECT statement. See the related topic "Creating a multi-line text area" to create a text box in which free-form text can be entered. ▶**ase** Grace needs to add additional colors to the list of choices and to change the pull-down menu into a scroll box.

10 Click the **WordPad program button** on the taskbar
Grace wants to add more T-shirt colors.

11 Place the insertion point after the word **Green**, then press **[Enter]**

12 Type **<OPTION>Teal**, press **[Enter]**, type **<OPTION>Orange**, press **[Enter]**, then type **<OPTION>Berry**
Now that the additional colors have been typed, Grace changes the pull-down menu into a scroll box by adding the SIZE attribute to the initial SELECT tag.

13 Place the insertion point to the right of the word **color** in the SELECT tag, press **[Spacebar]**, then type **SIZE=3**
Compare your document with Figure 4-11. Graces saves her work and switches to Netscape Navigator.

14 Click the **Save button** 🖫 on the toolbar, then click the **Netscape Navigator program button** on the taskbar
Grace refreshes her Web page.

15 Click the **Reload button** ⟲ Reload on the toolbar
The image is updated, as shown in Figure 4-12.

Grace decides to print the Web page.

16 Press **[Print Screen]**, start Paint (click **Start** on the taskbar, point to **Programs**, point to **Accessories**, then click **Paint**), then print your Web page.

This tip replaces Step 16.
16 Press **[Print Screen]**, start Paintbrush (open the Main menu, double-click the **Accessories program group**, then double-click the **Paintbrush application icon**), then print your Web page

FIGURE 4-11:
SIZE tag changes a
pull-down menu into
a scroll box

Number indicates how
many choices are
displayed in scroll box

Additional entries

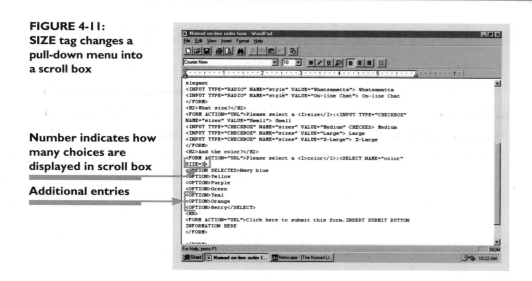

FIGURE 4-12:
Scroll box on a
Web page

Click to see
additional choices

Default selection

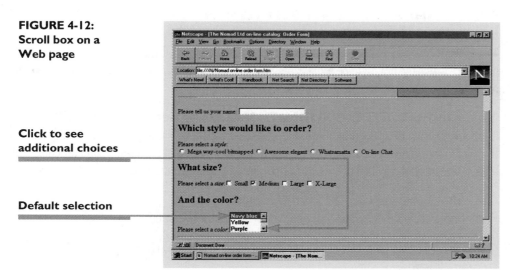

Creating a multi-line text area

As a courtesy to your Web page readers, you can add a comment section that per-mits them to type text in a free-form style. You create a text box using the TEXTAREA tag and options that control the height and width of the displayed box. For example, the box shown in Figure 4-13 was created using the following tags: <TEXTAREA NAME="comments" ROWS=5 COLS=40> </TEXTAREA>. By default, a 4-row by 40-column text box is created, but this can be modified, as shown in the tag.

Box automatically
scrolls as displayed
area is filled

FIGURE 4-13: TEXTAREA tags create a multi-line text box

TROUBLE?

If the items added to an <OPTION> list don't appear in your Web browser after clicking the Reload button, close the browser then reopen the file.■

QUICK TIP

If you don't remem-ber how to print a form using Paint, see the related topic "Printing a Web page" in the first lesson of this unit.■

Using push buttons with preset values

The information in a form is of little use if it is not sent to a Web address where it can be read or processed. In most cases, the data in a form is sent to a different URL address, and the easiest way to send data is to supply a push button on the Web page. The SUBMIT tag is designed to send form data to the server for processing. See the related topic "Supplying a Reset button" to learn how to use a push button to reset the default settings in your form. **case** Once the form is filled out, Grace wants customers to be able to send the information by clicking a single button.

STEPS

1 Click the **WordPad program button** on the taskbar
   Grace replaces a placeholder with information for the Submit button.

2 Select the **INSERT SUBMIT BUTTON INFORMATION HERE** placeholder
   The SUBMIT tag displays a default value on the face of the button that says "Submit Query," but Grace wants the button to be more expressive. She includes the VALUE tag that contains the message she wants to display on the button.

3 Type **<INPUT TYPE="SUBMIT" VALUE="Send data now!">**
   Compare your WordPad document with Figure 4-14. In a live Web session, the user would send the data to the designated URL, as determined by the Webmaster. This button has no function since Grace has not supplied its URL. Now that she's created the button, Grace saves her work.

4 Click the **Save button** 🖫 on the toolbar
   Next, Grace switches to Netscape Navigator and refreshes the document.

5 Click the **Netscape Navigator program button**, then click the **Reload button** [Reload] on the toolbar
   The document with the Submit button is shown in Figure 4-15.

   Grace is pleased with her work and decides to print the document.

6 Use the Print Screen button and Paint to print your Web page
   Happy with the results, Grace closes Netscape Navigator and WordPad.

7 Close Netscape Navigator and WordPad

onclick = "window. location. href =index. html' '">

FIGURE 4-14:
Creating a Submit
button

Creates a button type

Replaces default
button text

FIGURE 4-15:
Displaying creative text
on a Submit button

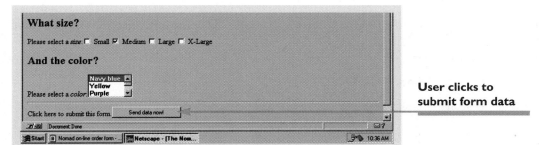

User clicks to
submit form data

Supplying a Reset button

Another common use of an on-screen button is to allow users to reset all the
default values for form fields. This feature gives the user a chance to "do over" all
the selections he or she has made. Like the Submit button, the function of the Reset
button is preset. By using the VALUE tag, you can replace the default "Reset" value
on the button face with any text you want. Figure 4-16 was created using the code
<INPUT TYPE="RESET" VALUE="Clear all entries!">.

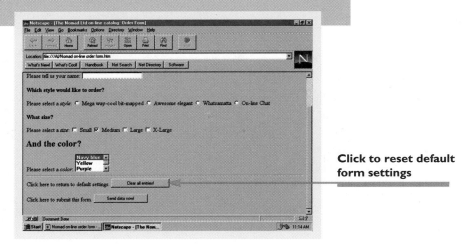

Click to reset default
form settings

FIGURE 4-16:
Reset button with
creative text

TASKREFERENCE

TASK	KEYBOARD
Add items to pull-down menu or scroll box	Type <OPTION>*option name*
Change pull-down menu to scroll box	Add SIZE=2 (or greater) to SELECT tag
Create a default checkbox or radio button item	Add CHECKED to INPUT TYPE tag
Create a default pull-down menu or scroll box item	Add SELECTED to OPTION tag
Create a pull-down menu	Type <SELECT NAME="*field_name*">
Create a single-line text field	Type <INPUT TYPE="TEXT" NAME="*field_name*">
Create checkboxes	Type <INPUT TYPE="CHECKBOX" NAME="*field_name*" VALUE="*field_value*">*displayed text*
Create multi-line text area	Type <TEXTAREA NAME="*field_name*"></TEXTAREA>
Create radio buttons	Type <INPUT TYPE="RADIO" NAME="*field_name*" VALUE="*field_value*">*displayed text*
Create Reset button with creative text	Type <INPUT TYPE="RESET" VALUE="*button text*">
Create Submit button with creative text	Type <INPUT TYPE="SUBMIT" VALUE="*button text*">
Define a form	Type <FORM=*options*>*items in list*</FORM>

CONCEPTSREVIEW

Label each element of the Netscape Navigator screen shown in Figure 4-17.

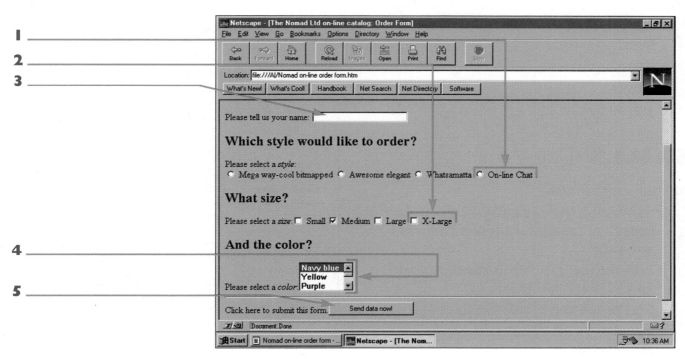

FIGURE 4-17

Match each statement with the HTML INPUT tag it describes.

6 Sends data to a specified location

7 Determines the kind of input

8 Creates a default selection

9 Determines the number of displayed items

10 Defines the field name

a. TYPE

b. NAME

c. SIZE

d. CHECKED

e. SUBMIT

Select the best answer from the list of choices.

11 Each of the following uses the INPUT tag, *except*

  a. checkbox

  b. scroll box

  c. radio button

  d. text box

12 Which tag changes a pull-down menu into a scroll box?

  a. SHAPE

  b. TYPE

  c. KIND

  d. SIZE

13 Which tag creates a multi-line text box?

a. TEXTBOX

b. SCROLLBOX

c. TEXTAREA

d. MULTILINE

14 The HTML tag that creates a button that returns a form to its default settings is

a. SEND

b. RESET

c. SUBMIT

d. RETURN

SKILLSREVIEW  *homework Done*

1 Create a text entry field.

a. Start WordPad, open the file HTML 4-2.htm on your Student Disk, then save it as Interstellar Pizza order form.htm.

b. In the blank line above "Who is ordering this pizza?" type <FORM ACTION="URL">.

c. Select the INSERT TEXT BOX HERE placeholder.

d. Type <INPUT TYPE="TEXT" SIZE=25 NAME="orderby">.

e. Press [Enter] then type </FORM>.

f. Save your work.

g. View your work in Netscape Navigator.

h. Use Print Screen to print your Netscape Navigator work.

2 Use checkboxes.

a. Return to WordPad.

b. Select the INSERT CHECKBOX INFORMATION HERE placeholder.

c. Type an INPUT TYPE="CHECKBOX" statement for a field named "Ptype." The VALUE field and displayed text information is shown in Table 4-4.

d. Make the Alien madness pizza the default value.

e. Save your work.

f. Reload the changes to the document in Netscape Navigator.

g. Use Print Screen to print your Netscape Navigator document.

| **TABLE 4-4** | |
VALUE Field	**Display information**
Szone	Safety zone
Sspecial	Surfer's special
Amadness	Alien madness
Prevenge	Planetary revenge

3 Use radio buttons.

a. Return to WordPad.

b. Select the INSERT RADIO BUTTON INFORMATION HERE placeholder.

c. Type an INPUT TYPE="RADIO" statement for a field named "topping." The VALUE field and displayed text information is shown in Table 4-5.

d. Make the pepperoni, onions topping the default value.

e. Save your work.

f. Reload the changes to the Netscape Navigator document.

g. Use Print Screen to print your Netscape Navigator document.

TABLE 4-5	
VALUE Field	**Display information**
Cheese	Cheese
Pepons	Pepperoni, onions
Ongarsa	Onions, garlic, sausage
Surprise	SURPRISE!!!

4 Use pull-down menus and scroll boxes.

a. Return to WordPad.

b. Select the INSERT PULL-DOWN MENU INFORMATION HERE placeholder.

c. Type a SELECT NAME tag for a field named "size."

d. Type an OPTION tag for each of the following sizes: 6 inches, 10 inches, and 14 inches.

e. Make the 10-inch size the default value.

f. Save your work.

g. Print the WordPad document.

h. Add an additional option to the list: "Surprise me!"

i. Change the pull-down menu to a scroll box by adding the SIZE=3 statement to the SELECT NAME tag.

j. Select the INSERT MULTI-LINE TEXT BOX INFORMATION HERE placeholder.

k. Type a TEXTAREA tag that creates a 4-row by 50-column text box for a field named "tellus."

l. Save your work.

m. Reload the changes to the document in Netscape Navigator.

n. Use Print Screen to print your Netscape Navigator document.

5 Use push buttons with preset values.

a. Return to WordPad.

b. Select the INSERT RESET INFORMATION HERE placeholder.

c. Type an INPUT TYPE statement for a Reset button that displays "Help - do over!" on its face.

d. Select the INSERT SUBMIT INFORMATION HERE placeholder.

e. Type an INPUT TYPE statement for a Submit button that displays "Order up!" on its face.

f. Save your work.

g. Use Print Screen to print your the WordPad document.

h. Reload the changes to the document in Netscape Navigator.

i. Use Print Screen to print your Netscape Navigator document.

j. Close Netscape Navigator and WordPad.

k. Submit your printed materials.

INDEPENDENT
CHALLENGE 1 *homework DONE*

Many of the Star Dot Star consulting firm's clients are avid World Wide Web users. In order to find out how many clients are using the Web, you've decided to add a questionnaire to your series of Web pages.

To complete this independent challenge:

1 Create a new WordPad document and save it as Star Dot Star customer profile.htm on your Student Disk.

2 Insert the logo file, stardot.gif, on the page. If you wish, you can reduce or enlarge its size.

3 To preserve your client's anonymity, create a text field for the client's zip code.

4 Create a series of checkboxes that asks the client how recently he/she has used your services. Some possible choices are last three days, week, month, year, etc.

5 Create radio buttons that let the client select the type of service he/she values most from your firm (such as consulting, repairing software problems, installing upgrades, etc.).

6 Create a multi-line text box for the client to provide optional free-form comments.

7 Print the document in WordPad.

8 Use Print Screen to print your Netscape Navigator document.

9 Submit your printed materials.

INDEPENDENT
CHALLENGE 2

To help rate the success of the Web pages you've designed for the Board of Realtors, they've asked you to develop a questionnaire that readers can answer on-line. The Board is interested in reader satisfaction with your Web pages, and how readers like the services performed by Board members.

To complete this independent challenge:

1 Create a new WordPad document and save it as BOR customers.htm on your Student Disk.

2 Insert the Board of Realtors logo file, realtors.gif, on your Student Disk anywhere on the page.

3 Create a series of radio buttons that determines the age bracket of the respondent (for example, 18–24, 25–34, 35–44, etc.).

4 Create a series of checkboxes that determines if the respondent currently rents or owns a home.

5 Create a pull-down menu that asks renters if their apartment is in a home or apartment complex.

6 Create a multi-line text box that lets clients describe the kind of property they are interested in purchasing.

7 Create a Submit button that sends the form data to a URL.

8 Save your work.

9 Print the document in WordPad.

10 Use Print Screen to print your Netscape Navigator document.

11 Submit your printed materials.

INDEPENDENT
CHALLENGE 3

Not only do the Film Clips customers love your Web pages, they've indicated a desire to tell you what videos they want so you can make better video purchases. You decide to add a questionnaire to your Web page that lets customers tell you what videos they want to see in the store.

To complete this independent challenge:

1 Create a new WordPad document and save it as Film Clips requests.htm on your Student Disk.

2 Create a text box in which the customer can enter his/her first and last name.

3 Create a series of radio buttons that lets the customer select a favorite type of movie, such as drama, action, documentary, or comedy.

4 Create a series of checkboxes that lets a customer choose black & white, color, or both types of movies.

5 Provide three text boxes in which your customers can enter the names of their favorite movie stars.

6 Save your work.

7 Print the document in WordPad.

8 Use Print Screen to print your Netscape Navigator document.

9 Submit your printed materials.

INDEPENDENT
CHALLENGE 4

Madam Zylog is interested in collecting information from her clients using a form on the World Wide Web. She's indicated to you that a person's date and time of birth is crucial information she'll need to make accurate projections.

To complete this independent challenge:

1 Create a new WordPad document and save it as Zylog customer form.htm on your Student Disk.

2 Insert the logo, zylog.gif, on your Student Disk in an appropriate spot on the form.

3 Create a text field in which a customer enters his/her date of birth.

4 Create a text field in which a customer enters his/her time of birth.

5 Create checkboxes for the customer to enter whether the time of birth was AM or PM.

6 Create a scroll box in which a customer can select his/her mother's birth month.

7 Ask the customer if they have ever been to another astrologer. The customer should be able to respond using "Yes" or "No" radio buttons.

8 Save your work.

9 Print the document in WordPad.

10 Use Print Screen to print your Netscape Navigator document.

11 Submit your printed materials.

VISUAL WORKSHOP homework

Use the skills you learned in this unit to create the Web page shown in Figure 4-18. Save your HTML file on your Student Disk in WordPad as a text document called Barbara's Bakery order form.htm, then print the document in WordPad and Netscape Navigator. The Barbara's Bakery logo is stored in the graphics file barbaras.gif on your Student Disk. Barbara's Bakery makes bagels in the following flavors: plain, onion, garlic, cinnamon-raisin, green chili, and sesame seed; the plain flavor is the default choice. Submit your printed materials.

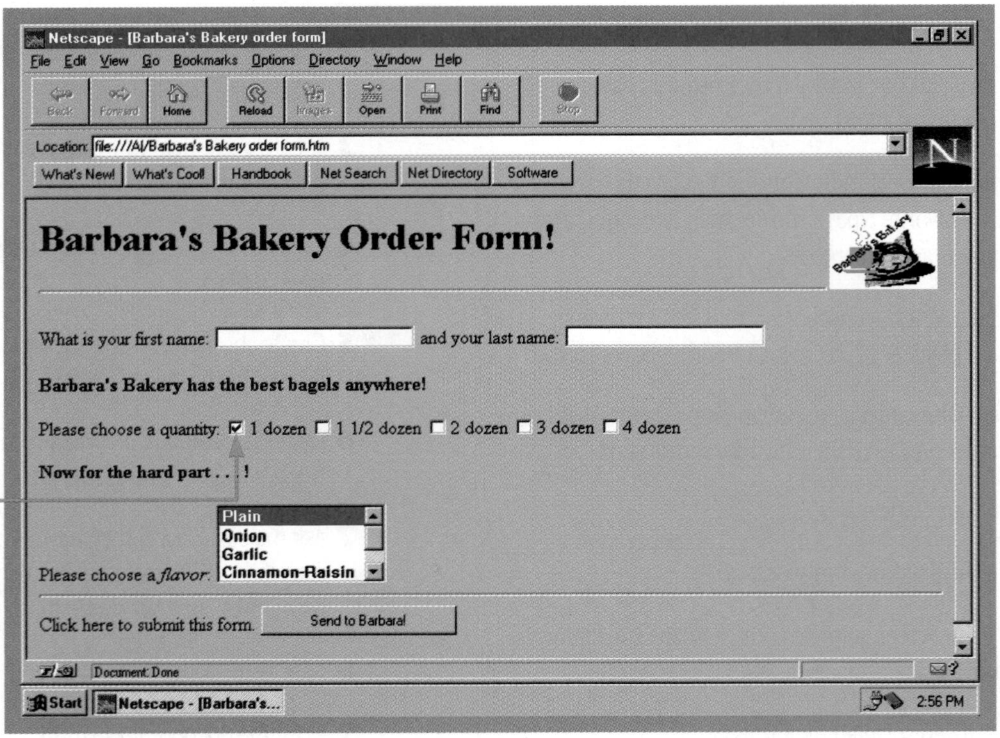

FIGURE 4-18

APPENDIX

Using
HTML RESOURCES

To create HTML documents for use in a business setting, it is important to know not only how to construct an HTML document, but also how to access and obtain helpful resources, such as an HTML editor, or multimedia files for your Web pages. Since you already know how to use search engines, such as Yahoo and WebCrawler, you have the knowledge needed to find information on the World Wide Web. ▶ Using a Web browser, such as Netscape Navigator, you can easily locate and use additional resources that are useful when working on the Web. ▶

Finding and downloading an HTML editor

The lessons in this book focus on teaching you which HTML tags to type to achieve a particular effect. Any text editor can be used—even your favorite word processor. An alternative to using a word processor and typing the HTML tags, however, is to use an HTML editor. With an **HTML editor** you can create HTML documents without having to type HTML tags. ▶ There are many HTML editors available; you can purchase one from a software vendor or download one directly from the Internet. ▶ Using a search engine, such as Yahoo, you can find many entries under "HTML editors." Figure A-1 shows the results of a search of HTML editors for Windows. Once you find an HTML editor that interests you, you can usually download the file from the program's Web site. Some editors are downloaded using an FTP site, as shown in Figure A-2. In other cases, the download process is started by clicking text or a button on a page, as shown in Figure A-3. Regardless of whether a file is downloaded from an http or FTP site, as the file is being retrieved, the Saving Location dialog box will display (if you're using Netscape Navigator) indicating where the file is being saved and when it will be finished. Once the file has been successfully downloaded, the Saving Location dialog box closes and you return to your browser. ▶ In most cases, your downloaded file will be a **self-extracting file**. Programs—even free ones—are so large and contain so many files that they are often compressed into one space-saving file. This makes transmission over the Internet easier and faster. Once the file has been successfully downloaded, locate it using the Windows Explorer (or File Manager, if you're using Windows 3.1). Then, double-click its icon to start the installation process. The single file will decompress and install automatically on your computer so it will be ready to use.

FIGURE A-1: Results of Yahoo search for HTML editors

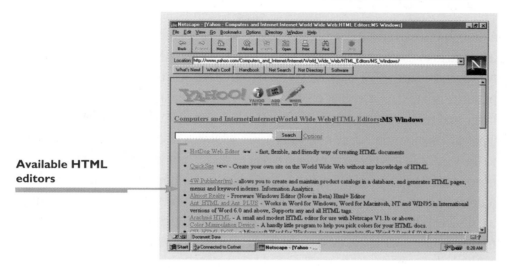

Available HTML
editors

FIGURE A-2: HTML Assistant Pro WWW FTP site

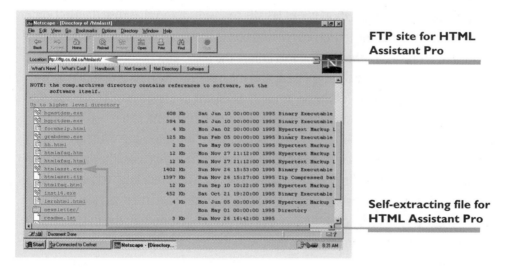

FTP site for HTML
Assistant Pro

Self-extracting file for
HTML Assistant Pro

FIGURE A-3: HotDog HTML editor Web site

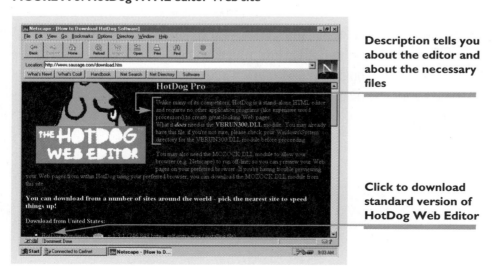

Description tells you
about the editor and
about the necessary
files

Click to download
standard version of
HotDog Web Editor

Using an HTML editor

Although you can create exciting Web pages using any word processor, the advantages to using an HTML editor are that you don't have to memorize and type the necessary HTML tags. Nearly all HTML editors let you insert tags by clicking buttons displayed on a toolbar or palette. This makes creating documents easier and faster, and reduces typing errors. ▶ The HTML Assistant Pro lets you select tags from a palette, as shown in Figure A-4. While you can always type HTML tags (as you did in the lessons in this book), it's much easier to click a button to insert the tags. In the freeware edition, shown in Figure A-4, the Table Assistant, Form Assistant, and Automatic Page Creator (which contain the basic tags necessary for every Web page) are disabled. These advanced features are available in the commercial version and make creating a Web page even easier. The HTML Assistant Pro also lets you open multiple documents, which are displayed in cascading windows. ▶ The HotDog Pro Editor—available for a free 30-day trial—has a welcome screen from which you can find out more information about HTML, follow its tutorial, or use the HotDog Pro Editor. The Welcome to HotDog! dialog box is shown in Figure A-5. When a new document is opened in the HotDog Pro Editor, the basic tags needed in an HTML document are automatically displayed, and the insertion point is positioned so you can begin typing the body of the document, as shown in Figure A-6. This editor also lets you open multiple documents and displays each filename at the bottom of the screen like worksheet tabs in a spreadsheet program. ▶ Choosing which HTML editor to use is largely based on personal preference. In most cases, they all function similarly. To enclose existing text in a container, such as a heading, you select the text then click the appropriate heading button. You can also insert a container *before* the text is typed by clicking the appropriate toolbar button; the initial and closing tags are inserted in the document with the insertion point in between them so you can type your text. Empty containers, such as <HR> or <BR> are inserted by clicking the appropriate toolbar button. ▶ Most HTML editors let you view your document off-line using any available Web browser. Instead of having to activate your browser and reload the file, you can use your HTML editor to test (in HTML Assistant Pro) or preview (in HotDog Pro) your document. This feature makes it easier for you to catch bugs in your document and ensures that your Web page works as it should *before* it's made available on the World Wide Web.

FIGURE A-4: Document displayed in HTML Assistant Pro

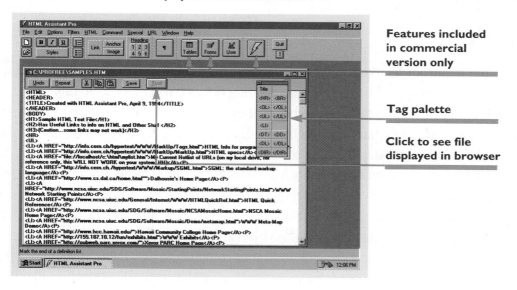

Features included in commercial version only

Tag palette

Click to see file displayed in browser

FIGURE A-5: HotDog Web Editor welcome screen

Click to use the editor

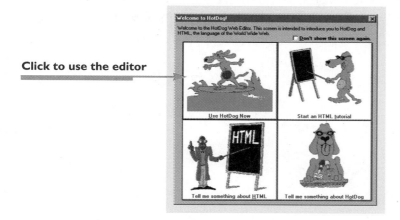

FIGURE A-6: New document in HotDog Pro

Chosen browser appears here

Basic HTML tags automatically displayed

Tabs for open documents appear here

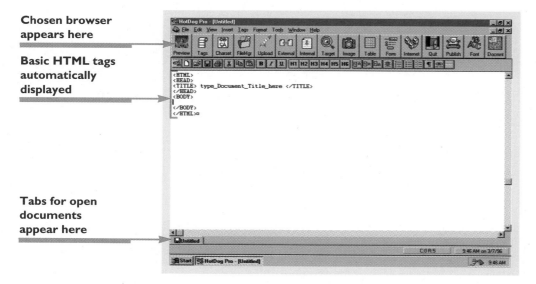

Finding and downloading multimedia files

You've already learned how to insert graphic images and multimedia files into a Web document, but you might be wondering how you can find files to use. Multimedia files on the Web—whether they're images, sounds, or movies—can be found through many creative means. In many cases, you can find multimedia files at a site related to a specific topic, or you can search directly for the type of multimedia files you need. Figure A-7 shows the results of a Yahoo search for video files. ▶ Using video files (movies) on the Web can be frustrating and difficult because video files are usually large and they require a long time to download. Viewing downloaded video files can also be tricky, since you need to have the correct viewer available on your computer to play them. If your viewer is not installed correctly, you might not be able to play the video files at all. ▶ Multimedia files are available on a variety of subjects, from home movies to animation using satellite imagery, as shown in Figure A-8. In most cases, video files available for downloading list exactly what kind of file format is being used and the size of the file, as shown in Figure A-9.

FIGURE A-7: Results of Yahoo multimedia video search

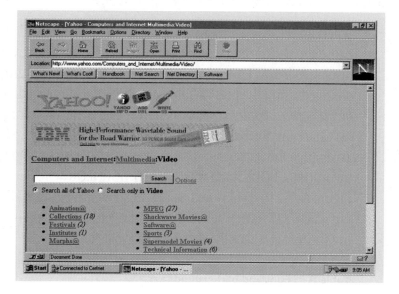

FIGURE A-8: Multimedia video sites for downloading

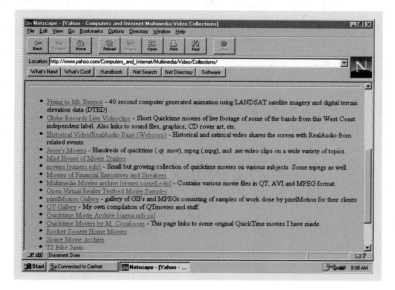

FIGURE A-9: Available video clips

Video format
displayed here

File size

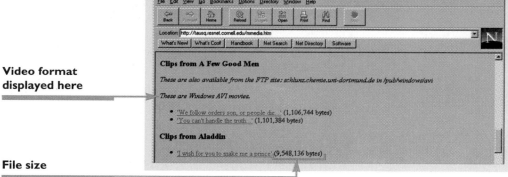

Adding color to a Web page

When an HTML document is viewed using a Web browser, the default settings cause the background color to display as gray and the text (or font) color to display as black. Fortunately, the color of the page background and text can be changed using the tags in Table A-1. ▶ Colors are typed into HTML tags using *hexadecimal triplet values*, as shown in the partial color chart in Figure A-10. ▶ Changing the background color of your page can give it a distinctive look. To change the background from gray to white, for example, you would replace the initial <BODY> tag with <BODY BGCOLOR="FFFFFF"> as shown in Figure A-11. To display text as red, as shown in Figure A-12, you would type the tag <FONT COLOR="FF0000"> to the left of the text; the </FONT> tag following the text changes the text back to the default color. ▶

Table A-1: Font and background tags

FUNCTION	EXAMPLE
Change background color	<BODY BGCOLOR="*value*">*body of document*</BODY>
Change text (font) color	<FONT COLOR="*value*">*text*</FONT>

FIGURE A-10: Partial color chart

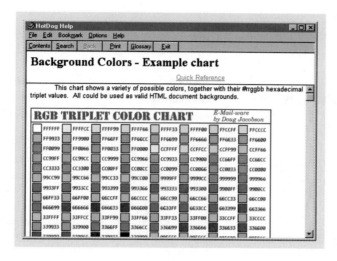

FIGURE A-11: Font and background color tags

Changes background color to white

Changes font color to red

Returns font to default color (black)

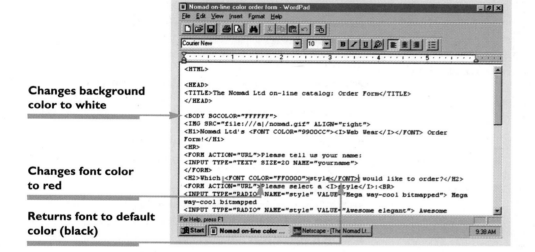

FIGURE A-12: Fonts and background color changed

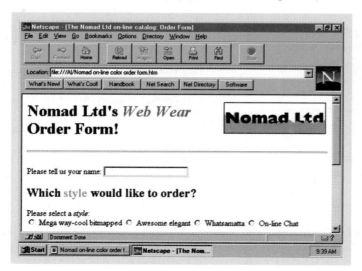

Glossary

Begins a comment line in an image map document.

/   Slash symbol replaces the backslash (\ ) symbol used in DOS; also denotes a closing tag.

| Pipe symbol replaces the colon (:) symbol used in DOS.

< >   Brackets; symbols that surround tags.

ALIGN   An optional code, physically aligns image on the page. Additional attributes HEIGHT and WIDTH are used to change the size of an image.

ALT   An optional code, precedes alternative text.

Attribute   Additional code that add qualities to existing codes.

Bulleted list   Each item in a bulleted, or *unordered list* is preceded by a dark, round circle. Each new line of a bulleted list item forms a hanging indent, in which the text is wrapped around directly underneath the previous text line.

Checkbox   Form device that enables a user to choose one item from many.

CHECKED   Determines default value; works only with CHECKBOX and RADIO. Commonly used codes, or attributes, used with a tag.

Containers   See tags.

Definition list   Displays a term or short group of words with an indented explanation underneath.

Directory list   Text displays in multiple-columns across a Web page.

Elements   See tags.

Empty container   An HTML code that does not require a closing tag.

Form   A method of collecting information for later use. A form can accept input from a user in the form of typed text, or by clicking the mouse on radio buttons, checkboxes, or labeled buttons.

GIF file   Graphics Interchange Format; developed by CompuServe. The most common natively supported graphic file format and works well when displaying images with small numbers of colors.

Graphic image   Electronic art files that are referenced in an HTML document and displayed by a Web browser.

Helper programs   Independent programs that let you use multimedia files.

Hot spot   Clickable area in an image that jumps to other Web locations.

HTML   HyperText Markup Language is a series of codes, sometimes called tags.

Hyperlink   Using HTML tags to reference another Web location.

Image map   Defines areas (or hot spots) within an image that are can be clicked to jump to other Web locations.

IMG   The image tag.

Inline image   A graphic file in a Web page that is aligned with text using special HTML tags.

INPUT   Creates the following form fields: single text lines, radio buttons, checkboxes, and Submit and Reset buttons.

ISMAP   An optional code; specifies that image is an image map.

Links   Connections to other Web site addresses (URLs) that are coded into an HTML document. Created using an anchor and hyperlink.

MAILTO   Attribute that allows readers to send e-mail with a single mouse click.

MAXLENGTH   Determines the maximum number of allowable characters.

Menu list   Items display left-justified one beneath another; they contain neither numbers nor bullets, and have no hanging indent.

Multimedia   Full-motion videos and sound files. Full-motion videos tend to have large files sizes and can be cumbersome on the Internet. Audio files have varying sizes.

MULTIPLE   Allows more than one selection to be made; displays as a scroll box.

NAME   Defines the name of the data; a required field.

Nested list   Lets you create expanded ordered and unordered lists by combining the <UL> </UL> and <OL> </OL> tags within an existing list.

Numbered list   Sometimes referred to as an *ordered list*, each line of text in the list is preceded by a number.

Pixel coordinates   Points within an image that are clicked; they can be identified using a variety of graphics programs.

Placeholder   Text (or objects) designed to be replaced at a later date.

Preformatted text   Text that displays exactly as it is typed in the HTML document; it can include enhancements, such as bolding and italics, and allows you to include your own line spaces and breaks.

Pull-down menu   Form device that enables a user to choose one item from many. Takes up less room than checkboxes or radio buttons.

Push button   Form device that has a preset function and performs a task.

Radio button   Form device that enables a user to choose one item from many.

Reload button   Used to refresh the current image in Netscape Navigator.

Scroll box   Form device that enables a user to choose one item from many.

SELECT   Creates scroll box and pull-down menu fields in a form.

SELECTED   Determines default value; works only with OPTION.

SIZE, IN A SCROLL LIST   Determines how many items display. If omitted, choices display as pull-down menu; if set to 2 or more, displays as scroll box.

SIZE, IN A TEXT BOX   Determines the size of the field; measured in characters.

SRC   The source tag; necessary when defining an inline image.

Tags   HTML codes; can be written in upper– or lowercase, are enclosed in brackets "<>", and sometimes occur in pairs (both before and after the text they surround). The ending tag differs from the beginning tag: it contains a / (slash) as the first character within the brackets.

Text box   Used in a form to collect information; a user types entries in a box, as in a paper form.

Text editor   Program that creates documents that can be saved in a text format, such as WordPad.

TEXTAREA   Creates a form field that accepts multiple lines of user text.

TYPE   Sets the input field to either "text," "password," "radio," "checkbox," "Reset," or "Submit."

VALUE   The value to be assigned to a choice; an optional attribute that doesn't have to have the same value displayed on the page.

Index